TITANIC

John Harper
God's man behind the legend

Victor Maxwell

Titanic - John Harper God's man behind the legend

ISBN 978-1-905989-30-0

Biblical BOOKS

Printed by:
Email:
info@jcprint.net
JC PRINT LIMITED

Contents

Preface

While studying in Glasgow in the early sixties I enjoyed worshipping each week at the John Harper Memorial Baptist Church. During my two years there it was an honour to be present when they marked the 50th Anniversary since the drowning of their famed and beloved pastor. Peter Donald was the pastor at that time. He was not only well respected for his preaching, but was also fondly remembered for skilfully playing his concertina. The Harper Memorial Male Voice Choir was engaged in their great ministry of praise. They made annual visits to the Festival of Male Voice at Templemore Hall in Belfast, Northern Ireland where I was pastor for nine years.

Another fifty years have gone by, and still the legend and legacy of Pastor John Harper lives on. His life and ministry served well to bless multitudes of people in Europe and America during his generation. His legacy is that of the passion and zeal he had to hold forth the Word of Life and point sinners to the Saviour.

The Bible says, "They that be wise shall shine as the brightness of the firmament; and they that turn many to righteousness as the stars for ever and ever" (Daniel 12:3). John Harper is counted among this great galaxy of soul-winners.

Our aim in producing this book is that the legend and legacy of Pastor John Harper should live on to bless and challenge generations to come. Much of the research gleaned for this book came from material in the public domain. We have, therefore, not only retold the story of the great preacher, but have dipped into the past to reproduce tributes and testimonies from his peers and colleagues in the book published in 1912, John Harper: A Man of God.

For that reason this preface is complimented by the original preface from John Climie in the aforementioned book.

Victor Maxwell

Preface (from John Harper: A man of God)

The editorship of this volume has been undertaken at the request of Pastor George Harper, who has rendered most valuable assistance, and whose tender and loving tribute to the memory of his brother will be read with special interest. As the biography is composed mainly of tributes by various writers it has been impossible to avoid duplication. But it has been considered proper that the tributes should appear as written, since each contributor writes from his own standpoint.

The tributes could have been greatly multiplied, and a larger volume issued. Many other admirers would gladly have given expression to their esteem for our departed brother, but it was thought better to produce a volume at a price that would suit the means of the working people among whom Mr. Harper mostly laboured, and who had conceived for him an extraordinary affection. He was a man greatly beloved, both for his own and for his work's sake. He lived in the hearts of the common people, and many were well-nigh inconsolable with grief when they heard of his sad end.

The sinking of the Titanic with its living freight had created a wail of sorrow throughout the civilised world. The idea of 1503 lives being lost through sinking of one ship is perfectly appalling. Even after the great ship was at the bottom of the sea, the newspapers, not knowing what had taken place, were announcing that the Titanic was "absolutely unsinkable." But the forces of nature were too much for the mammoth liner. The waters in the Polar regions had under the keen breath of the north wind massed themselves together, and from that ice zone came floating silently along the huge berg that ripped the steamer's bottom and sent it to the ocean bed. "By the breath of God frost is given: and the breadth of the waters is straitened" (Job 37:10). The iceberg straitened the Atlantic tract, and the great ship was sent to the bottom of the sea.

That Mr. Harper should have been taken away in his prime has perplexed many. We had ventured frequently within the past few years to predict for him a great future of usefulness, but

"We know not what awaits us,
God kindly veils our eyes."

Yet "as for God, His way is perfect" (Psa. 18:30). He could have hindered the Titanic from sinking, but He didn't. "He doeth according to His own will in the army of heaven, and among the inhabitants of the earth" (Dan. 4:35). "His ways are past finding out" (Rom. 11:33) . We reverently bow our heads under the shadow of this great calamity that has bereaved us of one who lived not for himself, but for the glory of Him who redeemed him with His own precious blood.

It is hoped that this small memento of a life lived for God and for the good of his fellow-men will carry a blessing with it, and be a stimulus to many. In this hope it is sent forth.

John Climie

197 St Andrew's Road
Glasgow

Launch

OF

White Star Royal Mail Triple-Screw Steamer

"TITANIC"

At BELFAST,

Wednesday, 31st May, 1911, at 12-15 p.m.

Admit Bearer.

1

Titanic: Queen of the Sea

For eleven years I was pastor at Templemore Hall in East Belfast. The church was built in the virtual shadows of the famous Belfast shipyards of Harland and Wolff at Queens Island. Sadly, it was during those eleven years that we saw the demise of what had been the largest shipyard in the world and the closure of the dry dock where the world's greatest liner, the *Titanic*, had been built.

Many of the workmen who engaged in the building of Templemore Hall were employed at the shipyard and had plied their trade to the building of the great *Titanic* and her sister ship, the *Olympic*. At its peak, the shipyard provided employment for up to thirty-five thousand people. With the passing of years those workmen have gone; the shipyards may be closed, but the fame and memory of the great ship lives on.

Ironically East Belfast has another link with the legend of the *Titanic*. Pastor John Harper from Paisley Road Baptist Church in Glasgow often visited the area to conduct evangelistic meetings. He was remembered for his fervent preaching and evangelistic skill. No one knew at that time that John Harper's name and quest for souls would be associated with the fate of the great ship which even then was being constructed by some of the very men who listened to his sermons.

Titanic's Launch

I can imagine the great celebration of thousands of those East Belfast workers and their families on that special Wednesday morning, 31st May 1911. Many of these had also been at Queens Island just over six months earlier to see the launch of *RMS Olympic* on 20th October, 1910. Now they had come to see the birth of the finest ship ever built and at 26,000 tons, the heaviest object ever moved by men. Thirteen minutes after midday the ship began to gracefully roll down the lubricated slipway and ease its way into the waters of Belfast Lough as the assembled crowd roared in applause and excitement. At that moment, one shipyard worker is reputed to have said with his typical Belfast humour and flippancy, "We just builds 'em, and shove 'em in!"

It took just sixty seconds for the giant hull to ease its way down the "slips". The great ship was then brought to a quick halt by huge clumps of anchor chains fastened to steel hawsers, which had been riveted to the hull's steel plating. These chains were soon detached, and the great *Titanic* was floating on salty water for the very first time, its almost empty hull riding high in the water.

The ship was as big as her name suggested, and the sight of her in the water was impressive and inspiring. The ship measured 882 feet long and more than 150 feet above the water line. Of course, the ship was far from complete. At this stage the *Titanic* was just a large hull, containing the massive engines and boilers. Over the next nine months thousands of men were busy turning the prize ship into the finished and luxuriant vessel she was designed to be.

Sadly, although it had been a memorable day of celebration, unknown to most of the cheering crowd, the launch of the great ship was overshadowed by a terrible tragedy. James Dobbins, a shipyard worker, who was knocking out shoring beneath the hull, was wounded by one of the falling timbers just as *Titanic* got underway. In an attempt to rescue him his fellow-workers dragged James clear. He was duly transferred to a nearby hospital, but sadly died from his serious wounds later the same day.

Perhaps this was a harbinger of things that were to come, but on that day negativity was unimaginable. The *Titanic* was not only the greatest ship ever built, but many people believed what one Belfast graffiti artist had written under the hull of the great ship: "Unsinkable".

Farewell to Belfast

On Tuesday, 2 April 1912, thousands of people lined the banks of the River Lagan and the Belfast Lough to watch the majestic liner *Titanic* smoothly move out into the open water. Smoke lazily filtered from its four funnels drifting into the morning air as the captain sounded the ship's horn to say a fond farewell to Belfast. Surrounding ships answered with ear-splitting blasts of their horns as humble tugs accompanied the new vessel out towards the Irish Sea. Under command of Captain Bartlett, the ship was subjected to several hours of sea trials before finally setting sail for Southampton.

The great vessel was now ready to assume her stately position as the queen of the sea. A voyage on board the *Titanic* was meant to be the experience of a lifetime, and it was a special honour to secure a passage on its maiden voyage from Southampton to New York.

All Aboard

The rich and famous of the day booked their places on the luxury liner to enjoy the unprecedented opulence of the pride of the White Star Line, the *Titanic.* Some nicknamed the ship, "The Millionaire's Special" while others called her "the wonder ship and the last word in luxury." The White Star Line had spared no expense in assuring the magnificence of this vessel.

For the maiden voyage the ship carried enough food to feed a small town for several months. This included sixty tons of fresh meat, fish, and poultry; forty tons of potatoes; 40,000 eggs; 7,000 heads of lettuce; over 100,000 pieces of fresh fruit and half a ton of grapes. It was also stacked with a ton and a half of coffee and tea and almost a ton of ice cream. There were 15,000 bottles of beer, 1,000 bottles of wine, and 8,000 cigars. All this bounty was taken on board for a journey that was to last for no more than five days.

Of course, not everybody on board the *Titanic* was necessarily rich and famous. Besides those who travelled in the extravagance of staterooms, others were in lesser accommodation in the lower decks of the ship going to America in search of a better future.

The ship's First Class quarters provided 416 cabins, staterooms and private suites of the highest standards for 905 passengers. Second Class passengers also benefitted from the high standards of accommodation, with meals that were on a par with first class levels on other ships. Even *Titanic*'s Third Class passengers enjoyed excellent accommodation with good meals.

That maiden voyage began just before noon on 10 April 1912 under the command of Captain Edward John Smith. Her first port of call was at Cherbourg in France and then on to Queenstown, near Cork in Ireland. Some people disembarked at Queenstown while others boarded the great vessel for the transatlantic crossing. At this stage no one could have envisioned what the next few days held.

On a fine Thursday afternoon, 11th April, again with crowds at the quayside to cheer her off, the *Titanic* loosed its moorings for the last time at Queenstown and headed out to the open seas coasting round the southern tip of Ireland. The White Star Line wanted this to be the fastest crossing of the Atlantic even though they had been warned about icebergs in the North Atlantic.

Passengers on all nine decks of the great ship were enjoying the superb voyage. Ladies kept diaries, others wrote letters while still more indulged in conversations with new acquaintances. On the bridge Captain Smith and his officers were making good headway and anticipated reaching New York in record time.

That Fateful Night

By Sunday April 14th, the *Titanic* had travelled some 1,400 miles and was east of Newfoundland. Just after 11.30 p.m. a lookout saw a large iceberg looming up ahead. The *Titanic* was heading straight for it at more than twenty knots per hour. On the bridge the officer swung the giant vessel to aft, but her fate was sealed. At 11:40 p.m. The great *Titanic* struck the iceberg with a glancing blow on its starboard side causing a 300 feet long gash in her side. A fireman compared the sound of the impact to "the tearing of calico, nothing more."

Nevertheless, the collision was fatal. The ship had been designed to stay afloat even if the front four water-tight compartments had been flooded. Alas, the iceberg had ripped open the first five compartments, and immediately icy water began to pour through the ship. Soon the pressure of the incoming icy waters began to split the plates on the *Titanic's* hull. The great "unsinkable" ship was doomed.

The captain and his officers on the bridge had to make quick decisions. Most passengers were asleep. Panic began to rush through the ship as quickly as the surging waters. Merriment and gaiety quickly turned to horror. Those who had retired for the evening were rudely awakened. Passengers rushed from their cabins to the open decks. Crewmen urged people to go to their muster stations. Other crew members began to lower the life boats to the icy and choppy seas dozens of feet below the decks.

At 12.25 a.m. the order was given to load the lifeboats with women and children, and by 1.15 am, seven had been lowered. An eyewitness reported: "They called out three times in a loud voice: 'Are there any more women before this boat goes?' There was no answer. Mr Murdoch called out, and at that moment a female came up whom he did not recognize. Mr Ismay said: 'Come along, jump in.' She said: 'I am only a stewardess.' He said: 'Never mind - you are a woman; take your place."

Elizabeth Shutes was governess to nineteen-year-old Margaret Graham who was travelling with her parents. As Shutes and her charge sat in their First Class cabin they felt a shudder travel through the ship. At first she was comforted by her belief in the safety of the ship, but her composure was soon shattered by the realization of the imminent tragedy. This is part of her record:

> Suddenly, a queer quivering ran under me, apparently the whole length of the ship. Startled by the very strangeness of the shivering motion, I sprang to the floor. With too perfect a trust in that mighty vessel I again lay down. Someone knocked at my door, and the voice of a friend said: 'Come quickly to my cabin; an iceberg has just passed our window; I know we have just struck one.'
> No confusion, no noise of any kind, one could believe there was no imminent danger. Our stewardess came and said she

could learn nothing. Looking out into the companionway I saw heads appearing asking questions from half-closed doors. All was deadly still, no excitement. I sat down again.

My friend was by this time dressed; still her daughter and I talked on, Margaret pretending to eat a sandwich. Her hand shook so that the bread kept parting company from the chicken. Then I saw she was frightened, and for the first time I was too, but why get dressed, as no one had given the slightest hint of any possible danger? An officer's cap passed the door. I asked: 'Is there an accident or danger of any kind?

'None, so far as I know', was his courteous answer, spoken quietly and most kindly.

This same officer then entered a cabin a little distance down the companionway and, by this time distrustful of everything, I listened intently, and distinctly heard, 'We can keep the water out for a while.'

Then, and not until then, did I realize the horror of an accident at sea. Now it was too late to dress; no time for a waist, but a coat and skirt were soon on; slippers were quicker than shoes; the stewardess put on our life-preservers, and we were just ready when Mr Roebling came to tell us he would take us to our friend's mother, who was waiting above.

No laughing throng, but on either side [of the staircases] and quietly, bravely, the stewards, all equipped with the white, ghostly life-preservers. Always the thing one tries not to see even on a ferry crossing. Now only pale faces, each form strapped about with those white bars. So gruesome a scene. We passed on. There were awful good-byes and the quiet look of hope in the brave men's eyes as the wives were put into the lifeboats. Nothing escaped one at this fearful moment.

We left from the sun deck, seventy-five feet above the water. Mr Case and Mr Roebling, brave American men, saw us to the lifeboat, made no effort to save themselves, but stepped back on deck. Later they went to an honoured grave.

Multitudes Overboard

It soon became obvious that many would not find safety in the lifeboats. Therefore, every passenger was issued a life jacket even though life expectancy would be short when exposed to water at four degrees below freezing. The last lifeboat containing forty-four people was lowered at 2.00 a.m. Hundreds of people were still on the deck as the water got higher and higher. The ship's orchestra was still playing *Nearer My God to Thee* as the ship began to list and tilt steeply.

As the bow of the ship sank lower and lower into the black murky ocean, passengers scrambled to the stern which was being lifted higher into the air. One passenger witnessed the sinking from a lifeboat. "We could see groups of the almost fifteen hundred people still aboard, clinging in clusters or bunches, like swarming bees; only to fall in masses, pairs or singly, as the great after part of the ship, two hundred and fifty feet of it, rose into the sky, till it reached a sixty-five or seventy degree angle."

With the bow section of the ship sinking lower into ocean the stern began to lift. At 2.18 a.m. the lights flickered and all electric failed so that the scene was enshrouded in darkness. People were scrambling to climb to the back of the ship which was slowly rising higher and higher.

At 2.20 a.m. the enormous pressure of the sinking bow abruptly broke the back of the ship and the stern lifted higher into the air. Suddenly, the bow of the *Titanic* plunged vertically into the icy depths and rapidly pulled the stern down in its forceful wake. So great was the speed of the descent of the ship that the *Titanic's* bow was embedded sixty-two feet into the ocean floor.

One survivor reported: "After she reached an angle of 60 degrees, there was a rumbling sound, which he attributed to the boilers leaving their beds and crashing down. Finally she attained an absolute perpendicular position and then went slowly down."

On that dark and moonless night despairing passengers fell overboard or jumped blindly from the sinking *Titanic* into the freezing and frenzied waters of the North Atlantic. Their shrieks of horror and despair pierced the night air and then quickly faded as one by one the pitiful victims succumbed to their inevitable fate. Even though they were wearing lifebelts they could not survive for long in the frigid sea.

Some despairing passengers in lifeboats vainly tried to retrieve the drowning souls from a watery grave. Only a few were rescued from the sea.

The Steely Facts

When the majestic *RMS Titanic* left Queenstown in Ireland there were 2228 people on board. Of these 337 were in first class accommodation, 285 in second class, 721 in third class and 885 crew members. These distinctions did not mean very much when the final passenger list was drawn up. The solemn 'saved' and 'lost' statistics showed that 1,523 men, women and children were 'lost', 705 people were 'saved'.

The Cunard Liner, *RMS Carparthia*, came on the scene at 4.00 a.m.

15th April 1912 and picked up the 705 survivors from the lifeboats and took them to safety.

Included amongst those who were 'lost' was Pastor John Harper of Scotland. Numbered with those who were 'saved' was Pastor Harper's six year-old daughter, Nina Harper. This book is about the glowing legend and testimony of God's man on the *Titanic*.

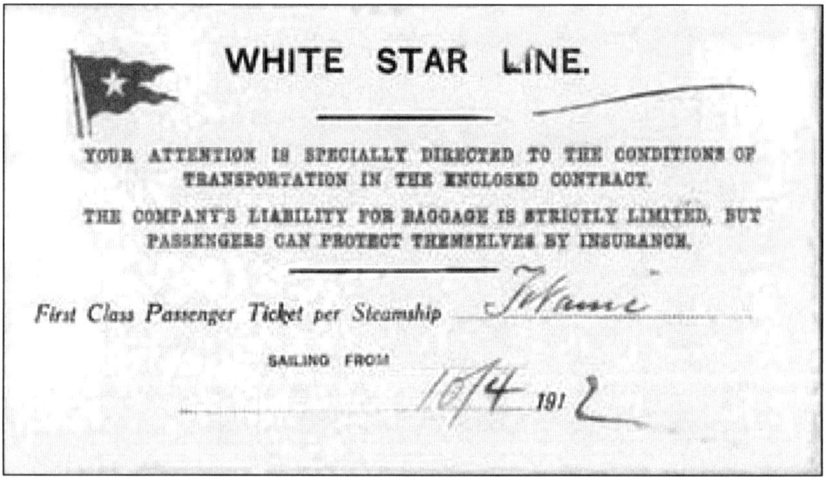

WHITE STAR LINE.

YOUR ATTENTION IS SPECIALLY DIRECTED TO THE CONDITIONS OF TRANSPORTATION IN THE ENCLOSED CONTRACT.

THE COMPANY'S LIABILITY FOR BAGGAGE IS STRICTLY LIMITED, BUT PASSENGERS CAN PROTECT THEMSELVES BY INSURANCE.

First Class Passenger Ticket per Steamship Titanic

SAILING FROM

10/4 1912

2

Titanic: Save Our Souls

Reports of the terrible disaster filtered through the air waves as wireless radio operators from the *RMS Carparthia* broke the news to the world. Within hours journalists around the globe printed their bold headlines, "Titanic Sinks Four Hours after Hitting an Iceberg".

The news soon gathered momentum and finally exploded like a bombshell to shocked families back home in Britain. Anxious relatives and friends gathered at the offices of the White Star Line in London and Southampton to glean any crumbs of hopeful news about their loved ones. Others were weeping and wringing their hands in despair to learn of the loss of a mother, a father, a son or a daughter and at times, even a whole family.

In Glasgow, Scotland, news of the disaster was greeted with grave dismay. The land of the thistle had produced many mariners, and quite a few of the crew members hailed from the city. All of them went down with the *Titanic*.

At Paisley Road Baptist Church in the Plantation area of Glasgow the congregation was dumbfounded to receive the news that their former beloved missionary, pastor and founder of the church, had lost his life on that fateful night on the North Atlantic.

The message they received was curt and to the point:

> Miss Leitch and Nan (sic) arrived well. Lost everything. When they were taken to the upper decks the women and children did not know it meant separation. No opportunity for farewells. We have no hopes Mr. Harper is rescued.

There was great lament that the young and gifted preacher would not be heard in Glasgow anymore. However, their sorrow was tempered with the great assurance of the gospel that although this beloved servant of God was lost at sea, they knew he was at home with the Lord.

They remembered him for his unabated zeal for the work of God and his passion for people. He often related his personal testimony of what Jesus Christ had done in his life.

John Harper

John Harper was born into a Christian home in the village of Houston, Renfrewshire, Scotland on 29th May, 1872. He was the youngest of five children born to George and Rachel Harper; Rose, George, Caroline and Alfred were his siblings. His father was a draper in the town.

Greatly influenced by his godly parents and their love for God and the church, young John Harper trusted Jesus Christ when he was thirteen years old. The verse that brought him to Christ was John 3:16; "For God so loved the world, that he gave his only begotten Son, that whosoever believeth in him should not perish, but have everlasting life." His salvation was an answer to his parents' prayers.

Being a Christian did not shelter John from adversity. Most of his life was dogged with tragedy. When he was yet a young boy he fell into a village well and almost drowned; however, he knew that God had spared his life for a purpose, and he wanted to prove that good, perfect and acceptable will of God.

When he was only seventeen years old and working long hours in a local paper mill, John was convinced that God was calling him to be a preacher. He frequently engaged in open-air evangelism on the streets of his own village. Baptist pastor E. A. Carter of the Baptist Pioneer Mission in London, recognised young John's gift and zeal for God's work and invited him to engage in their training course.

As part of that training John was assigned to the Govan district of Glasgow. As a result of his dedicated work and out and out enthusiasm as a city missionary John Harper founded the Paisley Road Baptist Church in 1897 with twenty-five members.

Under his pastoral care through the next ten years and as a result of his Bible ministry the Paisley Road Baptist Church grew from the original twenty-five members to a congregation of over 500 people. Because of this growth the congregation had to move to a new location on Plantation Street, near Govan.

Joy and Sorrow

28th April 1903 was a happy day for John when he married his sweetheart, Annie Leckie Bell. He looked on her as a helpmeet at his side and an extension to his ministry.

With the passing of time John Harper's ministry was gaining attention beyond Glasgow, and soon he was in demand as a preacher and evangelist in other parts of the British Isles and beyond. However, the preacher's life was overshadowed with tragedy and heart break. It is reputed that he almost drowned when he was swept out to sea. Also, while on a voyage he and his fellow passengers were stranded in the middle of the Mediterranean on a leaky ship.

However, none of these calamities could compare with the heartbreak John experienced in 1906 when his young wife died. The New Year had started so brightly when Annie gave birth to their daughter, Annie Jessie Harper on January 1st 1906. Sadly, their joy was short lived for Annie died just seven days later on 8th Jan 1906. She was laid to rest in Craigton in Glasgow.

It was a day of mixed blessings. On one hand he had lost his darling wife, yet he had gained an adorable baby daughter, Annie Jessie Harper, whom he would endearingly refer to as Nina although later she changed her name to Nan.

Samuel Rutherford, a fellow Scot of generations earlier, spoke of his hurt and adversity during the trials of his Christian ministry, "Oh, what owe I to the file, to the hammer, to the furnace of my Lord Jesus." Like Rutherford, the pressure of John's severe trials had a maturing effect on his life and ministry. Instead of diminishing his commitment to evangelism John embraced opportunities to enlarge his ministry. It was said that he would often spend the whole night pacing up and down the aisle of the House of God praying for the church members by name.

London and Chicago

That ministry was transferred to London (in proximity to Spurgeon's

Metropolitan Tabernacle) in 1910 when John Harper accepted a call to be the pastor of Walworth Road Baptist Church in the capital. The congregation at Paisley Road Baptist Church was sorry to see their pastor leave. At his last Sunday services the church was packed beyond its 900 seating capacity.

In 1911 Pastor Harper was invited by the great preacher Dr A. C. Dixon to the famous Moody Memorial Church, Chicago to conduct a series of evangelistic missions during November, December and January. So great was the impact of that mission that on notice of Dr Dixon's retirement, an invitation was extended to John Harper to return to Chicago for another three or four months of Bible ministry. Some believe that this visit was to invite him to be pastor at the Moody Memorial Church. Ironically, Dr Dixon was moving to Spurgeon's Metropolitan Tabernacle where he would pastor the church for eight years.

John, who at this time was still a widower at thirty-nine years old, decided to take his six-year-old daughter, Annie Jessie (Nan) and niece, Jessie Leitch, with him on the journey to Chicago. It is believed that Pastor Harper had originally made plans to sail on the *RMS Lusitania* of the Cunard Line, but he decided to wait a week so that they might enjoy the experience of travelling on the new ship of the White Star Line, the *RMS Titanic.*

The family travelled from London to Southampton to embark as second class passengers on the great ship for the transatlantic crossing. The sight of the great vessel must have been most impressive, and I am sure he was reminded that the stately ship had been made in Belfast where he had often conducted evangelistic meetings. The family boarded the ship and soon found their cabin. They unpacked and settled in for the six or seven day trip before going up on deck to explore and admire the grandeur and beauty of the colossal liner.

As the ship pulled out from the Southampton docks the two girls joined John Harper on deck to wave goodbye to the receding crowds of well-wishers. They were on their way. The ship made two brief mail stops in Cherbourg, France, and Queenstown in Ireland.

En route to Queenstown John wrote at least two letters which reveal his warmth, humour and zeal. The first was written on board on White Star notepaper to his dear friend at Paisley Baptist Road in Scotland:

> My Dear Brother Young,
>
> I am penning you this line just before we get in to Queenstown to assure you that I have not forgotten you and especially all your kindness while we were North. I intended sending on Mrs. Pratt's train fares just before I left but in the rush which was exceptional having had 11 or 12 services for the week-end I was unable to get it done. I will send it on from Chicago.
>
> We had a great season of blessing during the last few days in Walworth. I don't know how I am to thank dear Aunty Mary and yourself for all your kindness the Lord will repay you for it all.
>
> Trust things are going well at Paisley Road. The Warriors are with me here and are doing well so far on the journey.
>
> Very kindest love,
>
> Your loving auld Pastor John Harper

Another letter, also written on White Star notepaper, also shows his humour. The letter was posted in Queenstown on 11th April 1912:

> My Dear Mother Superior,
>
> I am penning this wee note just before we sail into Queenstown. The Warriors are with me and all of us are getting on well.
>
> Although they are with me you are not to think we are going to remain on the other side. Far from this we hope to be back in August and in Scotland in the autumn.
>
> We had a blessed time in Walworth during the last week. Quite a season of revival, I am confident there are going to be [piece missing].
>
> Remember me to all the moucher both auld and young and tell them they might each one of them write their auld Pastor a wee note and he will send them a post card.
>
> Kindest love to yourself and all of the clan.
>
> Your loving auld Pastor John

Iceberg on Starboard Side

After attending services aboard the ship on Sunday 14th April Pastor Harper, his daughter and niece had a quiet day. It was reported that later that evening Pastor Harper and Miss Leitch were standing on deck admiring the sunset. "It will be beautiful in the morning," remarked John Harper to his niece before retiring for the night. He did not know how telling and prophetic his words would be.

After the ship's collision with the iceberg sent a severe shudder through the ship, Harper awakened his little daughter, picked her up and wrapped her in a blanket before carrying her up to A Deck. There he kissed his darling girl goodbye before entrusting her to a crewman to put her on one of the lifeboats with Miss Leitch. John Harper left the girls so that he could go and help others.

The brave and selfless man sacrificed his own life to rescue others. Survivors said he went from the lifeboat, gave away his life jacket to another man because he thought it was more important for people who did not know Christ to be spared than for himself who had been a servant of God for many years. Those same survivors told how that Pastor Harper preached the gospel to all and sundry, especially emphasizing Acts 16:31, "Believe on the Lord Jesus Christ, and thou shalt be saved."

As the ship finally plunged to her watery grave John, with others, flung himself from the high deck into the frigid and dark waters beneath. The agitated sea appeared as though it was boiling as hundreds of people flailed their arms and tried to swim. Harper swam with purpose from one person to another asking the same pointed question, "Are you saved?" He repeated the same message as the apostle Paul had given almost two thousand years earlier, "Believe on the Lord Jesus Christ, and thou shalt be saved."

Pastor Harper's niece, Jessie Leitch, wrote a brief account later that month for the grieving people at the Moody Church in Chicago where her uncle had hoped to be ministering. The letter was misplaced and then rediscovered between two pages in the minute book for the executive committee of the Moody Memorial Church, near to their minutes for April 17, 1912. It reads:

About midnight Mr. Harper came to our stateroom and told us

that the vessel had struck an iceberg. While I was dressing he went to learn further particulars, and returned to say that the order had been given to put on the life belts. We did so, and, picking up Nan (sic) in his arms, he took her up to the deck. There the women were ordered to the upper deck. I had to climb a vertical iron ladder, and Mr. Harper brought Nan after me up to the ladder, and the men at the top lifted her up to me again.

There was no opportunity for farewell, and, in fact, even then we did not realize the danger, as we were assured again and again that the vessel could not sink, that the *Olympic* would be alongside at any minute, and that the women and children were to be put into the boats first and the men to follow, and that there were boats sufficient for all. Our boat was well manned- it was the eleventh to leave the vessel.

After about half an hour the *Titanic* went down. We were about a mile away, but even then I hoped and expected that Mr. Harper was in one of the other boats, many of which reached the *Carpathia* before ours did. How eagerly I looked for his face on the deck as we approached that vessel, but when all the boatloads had come aboard I feared the worst.

The last day we spent on the *Titanic* was Sunday. Mr. Harper asked me to read the chapter at our morning family prayers, and later we went to the Sunday morning services. The day was quietly and pleasantly spent, and when Nan and I went to look for Mr. Harper at about 6 o'clock to go to dinner I found him earnestly talking to a young Englishman whom he was seeking to lead to Christ.

That evening before we retired we went on deck, and there was still a glint of red in the west. I remember Mr. Harper saying,

> 'It will be beautiful in the morning.' We then went down to the staterooms. He read from the Bible and prayed, and so he left us.
>
> I caught hold of something and clung to it for dear life, the wail of the perishing all around was ringing in my ears.

Rescue the Perishing

Even in the icy water and before succumbing to a chilling death, John Harper did not lack courage and zeal. Several times in life he had already been confronted with drowning. Now the grave held no terror for John. With titanic selflessness he went from one victim to another, his voice carried over the waves by the gentle breeze as he cried out his Bible text, "Believe on the Lord Jesus Christ, and thou shalt be saved."

Of the half dozen survivors who were rescued from the icy waters that night, one of them was a young man John Harper had spoken to while they drifted among the debris. Four years later that same young man, a Scot like John Harper, rose in a meeting in Hamilton, Ontario, Canada, and declared:

> I am a survivor of the *Titanic*. When I was drifting alone on a spar that awful night, the tide brought Mr. John Harper, of Glasgow, also on a piece of wreck near me. 'Man,' he said, 'are you saved?' 'No,' I said. 'I am not.' He replied, 'Believe on the Lord Jesus Christ and thou shalt be saved.'
>
> The waves bore him away; but, strange to say brought him back a little later, and he said, 'Are you saved now?' 'No,' I said, 'I cannot honestly say that I am.' He said again, 'Believe on the Lord Jesus Christ, and thou shalt be saved,' and shortly after he went down; and there, alone in the night, and with two miles

of water under me, I believed. I am John Harper's last convert.

Before he finally went under the freezing waters John Harper was heard saying, "I am going down. I am going down." After a momentary pause he called out again, "No, no! I am going up."

With that the brave soul-winner was called to the Saviour's side. His body was never found. It sank to the depths of the ocean, but his spirit ascended to be with Christ which is incomparably better.

It is calculated that the inestimable fortunes of the rich and famous were lost when the great White Star ship plunged to her watery grave. For John Harper, loss was gain. He gained the crown of righteousness, which the Lord, the righteous judge, shall give unto all them that love His appearing.

John Harper's little daughter Nan recalled that she was sitting on her Cousin Jesse's lap when she saw the Titanic sink. She remembered watching the lights go out and hearing the screams of the drowning.

In New York, little Nan could not understand why her father did not come to her in this strange new land. "I left Papa on the big boat, and he told me to go with Cousin Jessie," she said. "Now I want Papa."

Her Papa never came. Nan and Miss Leitch returned to England a week later. When she was growing up, Nan was told not to speak about the terrible disaster. It was not until her later years that she started to speak about the sinking.

Nan went on to live a long life. She married the Rev. Pont of St. John's Rectory in Moffat, Dumfrieshire, Scotland. She died in 1986; her Cousin Jessie Leitch went to be with the Lord in 1963.

The family is now united with Christ. On the calm of that Sunday night John Harper had remarked, "It will be beautiful in the morning." Now they know just how beautiful that endless morning is on heaven's eternal shore.

The night before the "Titanic" sank Mr. Harper was seen earnestly seeking to lead a young man to Christ. Afterwards, when on deck, seeing a glint of red in the west, he said, "It will be beautiful in the morning".

"Beautiful in the Morning"

Oh, fair must it be in the morning,
When the sunset enkindles the west,
And the clouds, in their golden adorning,
Creep quietly down to their rest!
Rest we, like then, in the hope that a dawn
Calm and resplendent comes marching on.

Ah, drear is the tale of the morning,
And waesome the wail in the tide,
When the hand of the Ice-King, unwarning,
Tears open the vessel's side,
And into the depths of the ruthless deep
Thrusts multitudes fast in their final sleep.

Yet fair must it be in the morning,
If fair did the sun go down.
God's heroes, the death-trammels spurning,
Press up to the victor's crown.
Where then is thy victory, vaunting grave,
When ours is the Saviour, Mighty to save?

See, faithful to Christ, his Master,
Intent on the task He gave,
On the eve of the dire disaster
One is telling His power to save.
If sinks the sun with so pure a light,
It will rise again both serene and bright.

The death of the righteous who dieth
Is gateway to life evermore;
The joy that all glories outveith
For him is laid up in store.
Painless and tearless, with "no more sea,"
Beauteous indeed shall the morning be.

Horace E. Govan

Little Nanna Harper

John Harper

3

A Man sent from God

A friend's tribute - John Climie

It must be about twenty years, probably slightly more, since we first met Mr. Harper. Our earliest recollection of meeting him was in connection with his labours in the Gospel at Bridge-of-Weir. He then looked simply like a full-grown boy. But at that time, as all through his public career, the candle of the Lord burned brightly in his heart.

He was born in Houston, Renfrewshire, on 29th May, 1872, and it was on the last Sunday of March, 1886, when he was thirteen years and ten months old that he was led to Jesus. He never knew what it was to sow "wild oats". His young life from his early teens was moulded and shielded by his belief in the Lord Jesus Christ. The love of God was shed abroad in his heart, and it pervaded his life to its utmost circumference, shaping his thoughts, in due time spurring him to action, and preserving him from the evil that is in this world. It was through John 3:16 "For God so loved the world that He gave His only begotten Son, that whosoever believeth in Him, should not perish, but have everlasting life," that the way of salvation was made clear to his heart and mind. It has been the means of enlightening multitudes. It enlightened him, and freed him from fear. "Perfect love casteth out fear." He received the truth in the love of it, and the truth made him free. In the illuminating words of that text he saw Jesus as God's gift offered to the whole world, and therefore to him as one living in this world. He received that gift with thanksgiving, and for him a new era began. Those who conducted the public service at which he was led to the Saviour have been blessed to many, but such converts as John Harper are few and far between. There is sometimes great jubilation and multiplied Hallelujahs when some notorious sinner professes conversion, but often-times alas! the rejoicing is short lived. Some who have been much rejoiced over, have been afterwards found to be far from reliable. Whether there was any special rejoicing when the village boy that night trusted Jesus cannot be recalled, but in an honest heart, having received the Word, he kept it, and brought forth fruit with patience. The word of John 15:16 may well have been spoken of him, "I have chosen you, and ordained you, that ye should go and bring forth fruit, and that your fruit should remain."

It is not necessary that men should have plunged deeply into sin to be of special use for Christ after the saving grace of God overtakes them. Mr. Harper in the exercise of his public ministry could never tell of having wandered far from God, and far into sin. Yet under God he was the means of leading numbers to the Saviour who had gone far astray. From his early days he was by God's appointment, very manifestly, "a vessel unto honour, sanctified, and meet for the Master's use." It is to the Saviour's praise that He can, and that He does, change the lives of men who have disgraced and dishonoured themselves, and give them a place of honour and distinction in His service. But their deeds of darkness prior to conversation are sometimes a snare to them after conversion, rather than a help to them in service for Christ. A clean life before conversion is a valuable asset.

John Harper was born and brought up in a Christian home, as will be told elsewhere in this book. His parents, poor in this world, were heirs of the Kingdom which God hath promised to them that love Him. The more Christian homes there are the better, not only for the church, but for the nation as well. To be brought up in the nurture and admonition of the Lord, and in an atmosphere of prayer, and of reverence for the Word of God, is to be stamped in youth with impressions that are of great value, even though as is sometimes the case the results looked for are long in appearing. A godly upbringing is a priceless heritage. While it was on a Sunday night in March, 1886, that the boy in his fourteenth year was led to Christ there were all the impressions of the years that had gone before stored up in his youthful mind. It was for nothing that he had listened through these impressionable years to his father's prayers and pleadings, and expositions of the Word of God, in that humble home. The fuel had been laid on the hearth of his heart, and lo! on that Sunday night a spark of love divine fell on it, and the flame was kindled.

During the four years that followed there was nothing particularly noticeable about him, nothing at least that betokened or presaged the great usefulness that marked his future life. He attended regularly the Gospel meetings which were carried on with enthusiasm by some young men in the village, with the help of preachers from different parts. He kept himself free from entangling companionships, and in a quiet and unostentatious way kept the faith.

But after four years and four months, when he had just turned eighteen years of age, an enlarged experience was entered into. Growth is a law of the Kingdom of God. Sometimes it is very slow and scarcely perceptible. At other times it is phenomenally rapid. Some men grow more in an hour in the apprehension of the things of God than others do in years. Such a crisis has sometimes been called "The second blessing;" sometimes "The baptism of fire." By these and other terms preachers and writers have endeavoured to describe the marvelous change that has been suddenly manifested in the lives of some Christian men and women. But by whatever name the new experience may be called it is manifestly the Spirit of God working for growth in grace, leading the soul into a wider expanse, enlarging the horizon, clearing the outlook, implanting nobler ideals, making "young men to see visions, and old men to dream dreams."

It was in the year 1890 that John Harper got the vision that sealed him for public service. He was at home all alone one Saturday afternoon in the month of June. All around his village home nature was dressed in its best. June is the queen of the summer months. The flowers were blooming. The birds were singing. The sun was shining. But while other youths may have been roaming in the green fields, or by babbling brooks, inside that village home the Spirit of God was leading that young lad into green pastures and beside still waters. An enrapturing vision was given him, almost overpowering in its intensity, in which he saw and felt as never before the purpose of God in the Cross of Christ. In Christ's love for men as seen on Calvary he beheld anew, in fuller form, a door of hope opened for a sinning world, and along with that fresh revelation he felt that God was beckoning to him, and committing to him a part in the ministry of reconciliation. Next day his lips were opened. Taking his stand on the street of his native village he began to pour forth his soul in earnest entreaty for men to be reconciled to God.

Any education he had received was obtained at the Board School in his native village, and like many other boys he was not too eager for school lessons. He was anxious to get to work, thinking like others of his age that work is the mark of manhood. Besides, anything he could earn was needed at home. As soon as he could get away from school his hands were filled with labour. He worked at gardening for a little, but he was at work in a paper mill when he received the fresh anointing, and the call to service. No university ever got the opportunity of shaping him. He came from God's Hand for service with no college stamp upon him. This may have lessened his status in the eyes of some, but it did not lessen his zeal for the moral and spiritual welfare of his fellow men. And after all it is not what a man acquires in scholarship, but what a man accomplishes in result that counts among right-thinking men. He had an orderly mind. This became more noticeable as the years went by, and he was a diligent student of theological works. As a lad he had imbibed a good deal of what is known as Calvinistic doctrine, but of the very rigid, narrow type. However, as he grew in grace and in knowledge, his mind broadened, and he found no difficulty in holding fast any truth or system of doctrine whether termed Calvinistic of Arminian that seemed to have Bible support. Divine Sovereignty and Free Will, as these terms are popularly understood, he embraced and held fast to, believing them to be rooted in the Word of God. How they co-exist he didn't profess to be able to explain, and he didn't argue about them, feeling as the wisest and devoutest of men in all generations have felt that they are matters for faith, and not for discussion. He was an eager Bible student. He read the Sacred Book. He meditated upon it. He used any commentary that would throw light upon it, or that would help him to draw light from it. He yielded himself to its sway. He expounded it. Few could make better use of it than he "for doctrine, for reproof, for correction, for instruction in righteousness." Whatever form of doctrine was found in it he adhered to. This he did tenaciously. He took fast hold of what instruction it gave him. He esteemed it as his life. Whatever doctrine was not found in the Holy Scriptures, it mattered not how fancifully put, not by whosoever it was proclaimed, found no place with him. "Thus saith the Lord" was his stand-by. He stood on the rock of revelation. Men's theories to him were sand. God's Word was rock. He constantly proved its worth, and he was not ashamed to avow his faith in it. He often quoted texts in an impressive way, and men would remember the text he preached from even if they remembered nothing else. A gentleman in business in Glasgow remembers seeing him get up in a hall in Kilbarchan about twenty years ago and quote I John 1:7, "The blood of Jesus Christ, God's son, cleanseth us from all sin." The words "all sin" were repeated by him three times over, each time with growing emphasis. "There's something in that, lad," the gentleman said to himself. Most assuredly there was, and in due season that "something" was seen.

When God is needing a man for His service He knows where to look for him. He scans the field. He sees the need. He chooses the man. He called Elisha from the plough; Amos from the flock; Peter from his fishing boat on the shores of Galilee; and John Harper from the paper mill. And when God puts a man into a berth nobody can give him his "walking ticket." Room will usually be made for him when the gift and calling of God are manifest, and if no room can be made for him in the Church until he is proved and tested and his fitness seen, God will find for him a sphere of service in which to manifest the divine call.

In service for God labourers are always needed, men who are willing to toil and suffer, to spend and be spent, to bear reproach, and endure hardness, as good soldiers of Jesus Christ. John Harper was a labourer – a labourer together with God (I Cor. 3:9), a man who put heart and soul and strength and mind into every bit of service that he rendered. At the outset of his career he dreamed of no church pulpit. If he found an empty street corner when he went anywhere he filled it. That was his pulpit, and he made full use of it. All round about the district where he lived, after receiving the special enduement of power from on high, he went preaching the story of redeeming grace. Bridge-of-Weir, Kilbarchan, Elderslie, Johnstone, Linwood, and elsewhere would find him at night after his day's work was over, heralding forth with youthful hopefulness the story of God's love to men. His heart was all aglow. He did one thing then, and he did it to the end – he laboured to bring men from sin to God.

This is work that must go on, "The story must be told." Wanderers from God must be followed, warned, pleaded with, and prevailed upon to break with sin and follow Christ. If one of God's servants is taken away, somebody ought to be ready at the divine call to step in and fill the gap. Not necessarily to serve in the same sphere, but to keep alive the same testimony. The number of witnesses must not be thinned down. The world needs the gospel today as much as ever. The blood of Jesus is as efficacious as ever. The Spirit of God is as much present as ever, yet alas! it may be that He is so deeply grieved that His power is less in evidence than it would be. There must be work while it is day. This is the day of salvation. The night cometh when no man can work.

After five or six years of earnest, consistent Gospel service, toiling in the mill during the day, and in the rural districts around pleading with men at night to prepare to meet their God, Rev. E.A. carter of the Baptist Pioneer Mission, London, "discovered" the young village preacher, and set him free to devote his whole time and energy to the work so dear to his heart. Under the auspices of the Mission, a Baptist cause was begun in Govan, one of Glasgow's neighbouring burghs, where there was plenty of elbow room for aggressive work. For some time mission services were carried on, then a Church was formed. The opening service was conducted by Pastor J.B. Frame, and next day a sermon was preached by Principal Macgregor of Dunoon College, on the words: "There was a man sent from God whose name was John." The text may have provoked a smile, but it was suitable for the occasion. In that hall there was present a man who beyond all doubt, as after results proved, was sent of God, and his name was John. It is a great thing to be sent from God. The credentials he had with him were the signs that God had already wrought by him. He had no others. But these were sufficient to encourage the belief that God had sent him. Though young in years he already had a creditable record behind him. The seal of God had been set on his service in the scattered districts were he had witnessed a good confession, and now in the midst of a teeming population it was believed he would be more useful than ever These hopes were not belied. When God sends a man He supplies all needed grace. No good thing does He withhold from them who walk uprightly in the path of service to which He calls them. Men sent from God with a Gospel message are made the custodians of a power that converts sinners from the error of their way. But if men run before God sends them, such results will not appear. In Jeremiah's day God made complaint through him of those who spoke "a vision out of their own heart, and not out of the mouth of the Lord" (Jer. 23:16), Of them he said: "I have not sent these prophets, yet they ran; I have not spoken to them, yet they prophesied. But if they had stood in my counsel, and had caused my people to hear My words, then they should have turned them from their evil way, and from the evil of their doings" (Jer. 23:21-22). This is a description of un-sent men. Their message is from their own heart. It is not from God. They stand not in God's counsel. They turn none of the people from evil ways, and evil doings. A God-sent man will speak forth the Word of God. Not a vision from his own heart will he declare. The result will be that men will turn from their evil ways, and bow in penitence and adoration at the feet of Him, the once-crucified, but now-glorified Saviour. Under John Harper men turned from their evil ways and evil doings. They forsook uncleanness and followed after holiness without which no man shall see the Lord.

It may have seemed a matter of small movement in the eyes of some, the setting apart of that young man for Gospel ministry that day. But hundreds upon hundreds have reason to bless God that they ever saw his face or heard his voice. For about eighteen months he toiled incessantly in Govan, plodding, praying, preaching, pleading, touching the hearts and lives of some with his earnest appeals, and gathering about him a small company of men and women who saw in him the marks of a God-sent man.

In the early days of his work in Govan one of the members of an evangelistic band was sent as a deputy from the city to speak at a mission service in Govan. When he got to Govan Cross he saw a young man standing there "preaching for all he was worth." "Who is that?" he said to a man who was with him. "That is the Baptist Mission preacher," was the answer. The impression made that night, and deepened afterwards by further acquaintance with the young man who was "preaching for all he was worth," as he has expressed it, led him into fellowship in the Church when it was formed, and made him ever afterwards one of Mr. Harper's staunchest friends.

After a year and a half of service in Govan a move was made to Gordon Halls, Paisley Road. Here on 5th September, 1897, a Church was formed of 25 members, some of whom had come with him from Govan. The Church was named Paisley Road Baptist Church, the name it still bears. But it has been suggested that it should now be called the Harper Memorial Church.

Men and women of all ages gathered round the young preacher, and with him as leader, work was carried on in no formal manner. At all the inside meetings increasing effort was made to win men to Christ. Outside, meetings were held at street corners, at the gates of public works at the meal hours, and wherever a hearing could be obtained. The net was cast on every side. The zeal and enthusiasm of the workers seemed boundless. Such were won, the cause prospered, the membership was increased. The faith which worketh by love and is radiant with hopefulness, animated the workers, and led them on from victory to victory over the forces of unbelief.

After four years in the Gordon Halls a site was got in Plantation district, and in an iron building, capable of seating five or six hundred people was put up. To it as a centre the work was transferred, and within its walls marvelous things were seen of God's saving power. A continuous stream of pardoning mercy poured itself though the services, and six years ago the building had to be enlarged to make room for the increasing demands of the work. It is situated in the midst of a teeming working-class population. No person living, however closely associated with the work which was carried on can ever know anything fully of the amount of good which was accomplished by Mr. Harper's ministry.

The superintendent of a large evangelistic hall in Glasgow was visiting some time ago an old man in High Street, fully two miles away from Paisley Road Church. The old man who is in his 80th year, was asked if he was trusting Jesus. At once he answered in the affirmative. On being asked how long it was since he trusted the Saviour, he said, "Nine years." "What age were you, then?" "Just turned 70." "And how did it come about?" "Well, I was passing Plantation, and yon man, Mr. Harper, was preaching in the street corner, and I trusted the Lord there and then." In and around the district in which the Church is situated, there are many, many homes that have been blessed, brightened, beautified, by the preaching of the Lord's servant, whose sad end so many mourn. The Church that was formed with 25 members had a membership of nearly 500 when, after 13 years' service, he left in September, 1910, to take up duties of the pastorate in Walworth Road Church, London. The farewell meeting was a most memorable one. The iron building, seating about 900, was quite inadequate to take in all who desired to attend, and the use of a large U.F. Church in the neighbourhood was kindly granted for the occasion. It was crowded to excess.

He was always an earnest preacher. Never a trifler. Never a mere retailer of addresses. He was ever a man who had his gaze fixed on the need of precious souls. But during the later years of his ministry in Glasgow his preaching seemed to take on a higher note. There was a consuming earnestness that grew with the passing years. His preaching power on occasions was something extraordinary. This was not merely when appealing to the unsaved to be reconciled to God, but also when exhorting the children of God to higher things. Without doubt, as those of us who knew him well can testify, the passionate, vehement longing that found expression in his public utterances had its well-spring in the seasons of prolonged supplication to which he gave himself. He was pre-eminently a man of prayer. Barely one month before his end when in Glasgow on a visit he spent half an hour with a few of us over a cup of tea, and the last word we remembered him saying was that the need of today was a deeper prayer life.

His brief ministry at Walworth Road was very signally blessed of God. Progress was made. The church membership increased. Everything looked hopeful. New ties of interest were formed. New friendships were made. Then came the invitation to conduct special services in the Moody Church in Chicago during the past winter.

References to that notable work appear in the later pages of this volume. When he came back to London in January it was not thought that he would agree to pay a return visit so soon as he had arranged to do. But he was going off "early in April," he said to us a fortnight before he sailed.

"Why are you going back so early? Surely not again to conduct special services?"

"Oh, no," he said, "I am going to conduct the regular services in the Moody Church, and speak at conferences and other gatherings elsewhere."

Full of hope he set out on the ill-fated steamer, and met his doom on the way. Is that what we should say? Should we not rather say that he met his Lord on the way?

On that fateful Sunday night just an hour or two before the Titanic struck the iceberg, he looked at the sky and seeing a glint of red in the west, he said,

"It will be beautiful in the morning." Yes, so it would, but the beauty that would break on him was not that which he was alluding to when he spoke these words. The beauty of the Saviour he would see.

After a very brief married life he lost his wife early in the year 1906. Their little daughter, Nana, is now a few months over six years old. The blessing of the Lord will surely rest on the little orphan girl. "A Father of the fatherless... is God in His holy habitation" (Psalm 68:5).

[illegible] APRIL 16, 1912.

THE TITANIC SUNK.

COLLISION WITH ICEBERG.

1,500 LIVES LOST.

WIRELESS CALLS FOR HELP

LINERS TO THE RESCUE.

The maiden voyage of the new White Star liner Titanic ended in disaster yesterday morning, the giant vessel sinking, with about 1,500 of those on board, off the coast of Newfoundland, after collision with an iceberg.

The news of the collision was received on the night of the 14th inst. in Montreal by wireless telegraphy, and several Atlantic liners also picked up the Titanic's messages calling for immediate assistance.

The Virginian, Parisian, Baltic, Olympic, and other vessels proceeded at full speed to the damaged liner, and over 600 of the passengers were subsequently transferred without mishap. It is officially stated that many lives have been lost.

TITANIC LOST

Unparalleled Shipping Calamity

TRAGIC COLLAPSE OF A MAIDEN VOYAGE

REPORTED LOSS OF OVER 1,600 LIVES.

WOMEN AND CHILDREN SAVED.

675 Rescued by Lifeboats.

GRAPHIC DETAILS.

George Harper

4

A Man Greatly Beloved

My brother as I knew him - Pastor George Harper

The scene recorded in the closing verses of the first book of Samuel, and in the opening verses of the second book, gives us a vivid picture of a day of disaster in the history of Israel. Among the many slain by the Philistines on Mount Gilboa was a young man named Jonathan, the son of Saul, the king. Doubtless Jonathan was considered by many in Israel as the coming man. The time could not be far distant when he would occupy the throne, and would go before the armies to battle, leading them in triumph against their enemies. To many, doubtless, he was Jonathan the valiant, the brave, the fearless, the trustworthy, and why? Because he was Jonathan the good.

Little wonder, then, tears were shed in Israel, when it became known that Jonathan was among those who had fallen. In all likelihood, as men talked with one another, they would pay tribute to the memory of one so full of promise, so good and true. There was in Israel at that time a man upon whom the disaster to the armies of his people at Mount Gilboa, and especially the death of Jonathan, had fallen like a crushing avalanche of deep, dark sorrow. Such an one was David. But notwithstanding his tear-dimmed eyes and bleeding heart, he too sought to lay his tribute upon the memory and name of Israel's prince, who had so honourably fallen in battle. Hear his words, "O Jonathan, thou wast slain in thine high places, I am distressed for thee, *my brother*, Jonathan: very pleasant hast thou been unto me: thy love to me was wonderful, passing the love of women" (2 Sam. 1:26).

Ah! Others might speak of Jonathan's excellent qualities, and rightly too, but it was reserved for David to speak of him as "my brother". Such is my position here. To me, Pastor John Harper, who sank with other fifteen-hundred and three persons in the never-to-be-forgotten *Titanic* catastrophe on 15th April, 1912, was *my brother* in a double sense, in the flesh and in the Lord. Not only so, he was my only bother in the flesh. Together we were brought up, together we bowed at the family altar, as our godly father

"...Kneeling down to heaven's eternal King;
The saint, the father, and the husband prayed."

Together we slept as boys in the same room, together we went to school, together we fished for trout in the little burn that flowed not far from our cottage home. Together we sat in the village church, and with but the brief space of three months between, I may add, together we entered the heavenly pathway, and as the years rolled on we kept step in our beliefs and convictions, in matters spiritual, sharing our joys and sorrows in every possible way. The great ingathering of precious souls into our Lord's Kingdom, which my dear brother witnessed in Chicago last winter, afforded me unbounded joy. Surely, then, my text will not be grudged me when I quote it, "I am distressed for thee, my brother John: very pleasant hast thou been unto me; thy love to me was wonderful, passing the love of women."

The earliest recollection of my boyhood days is associated with an accident that befell my brother. We had been playing some little childish game beside the rather deep spring well at the end of our garden, when John missed his foot and tumbled into the well. He was then only two and a half years old. What could I do? Only one thing, stand at the top of the steps and cry "Mother, mother," for all I was worth. Mother came to the rescue just in time to save John's life. I well remembered how she held his feet up in the air, and how the water flowed from his mouth. I admit it was a somewhat primitive method of resuscitation, but it was mother's method, and it proved to be successful. Nearly drowned at two and a half! Twenty-four years later we were working together in special mission work as "The Harper Brothers". The day was very fine, we were some miles from Barrow-in-Furness, on the coast. Without considering the possibility of a strong receding tide, we entered the water to bathe. I could swim but a very little, John could not swim one stroke. We were soon in difficulty, but for that Providence which rules all, my brother's life-story might have ended in the sea, and mine too, on that occasion. When once we got safely out of danger, we felt, exhausted though we were, sure that our Heavenly Father had mercifully saved us, and together we praised Him. Six years after this, when on a trip to Palestine, in company with his personal friend, Mr. Wylie of Glasgow, they were on board a ship on the Mediterranean which sprang a leak. After hours of weary suspense, most of which time they were face to face with death, they were rescued. My brother, in a lecture afterwards graphically described this incident. He said, "The fear of death did not for one moment disturb me. I believed that sudden death would be sudden glory, but, there was a wee motherless girl in Glasgow, and, oh, I thought, if I had only committed her to my dear brother George's care before I left." Needless to say, his brother would unhesitatingly have accepted the trust, whether committed to him or not, a trust he would have considered sacred. Thus on three occasions to my knowledge, prior to the final one on 15th April, 1912, my brother was face to face with a grave in the waters.

But, returning to those early days again, did space only permit, one could recount many very interesting incidents. At school my brother was somewhat careless. I don't recollect how far he got on in class work. He certainly, in those early days, did not make all he might have made of his opportunities at school. Our parents were humble people. My father had a drapery business in the village of Houston, which did not yield a large income, but notwithstanding the problem of bringing up six of a family, he strove to give us all the best possible education. My father was himself a man of fair education, and was widely read. However, John was not mindful in those days, and missed much that would have proved helpful to him in after years, as he often admitted. I think the marvel is that he developed so strikingly. Again and again his diction in address, and in letter-writing was, to me, simply charming. But, from his later teens onward he was a laborious student, few men prepare themselves and their message for the pulpit as he did. This, perhaps is, at least, one explanation of my brother's development.

I well remember our school-master calling John out for punishment. It may have been because of his badly-prepared lessons. I rather think it was. However, the cane was being used somewhat freely and severe. I sat for a short time, then my stronger self-asserted itself. In those days, as in all the intervening years, my bother was the apple of my eye. Accordingly I felt within myself, this will not do, lessons or no lessons, this man will not beat my brother after such a fashion. I rose, with my slate in my hand, which I raised above my head, declaring at the same moment, "If you don't stop flogging my brother, I'll do for you." He stopped at once, and came right up to me, and before the whole school praised me for thus standing up for John. Ah! don't you see, John was *my brother.*

School days were all too soon over, and as stated by others, John went early to work. It was not considered in those days in the country wrong to send a boy to work at the age of fourteen or fifteen. He was supposed to have got a fair education, and to have got some bone. For five years or more he followed various occupations, as told elsewhere. It was at the beginning of this period in his life that he was led to Christ. I well remember the evening. It was on the last Sunday in March, 1886, that dear John was born of the Spirit. The way had been well prepared for this. My father was a man among men, as my esteemed friend, Mr. Hugh Morris, points out in his tribute. He was a Puritan in theology and in practice, a man who loved his Lord and his Bible. A great admirer of C.H. Spurgeon, whose sermons he constantly read, and that aloud too and to which, at stated times we had all to listen, whether we enjoyed them or otherwise. Family worship, with the careful reading of the scriptures, and prayer, in conjunction with which we sang together one of David's Psalms, was the order of our cottage home. In this Puritanic atmosphere our family were cradled. John was thus ready in a very real and practical manner for the great event in his life, viz., his surrender to Christ. Mr. Walter B. Sloan, and Mr. Archibald Orr Ewing, both now of the China Inland Mission, occupied the village Free Church pulpit that evening. My dear brother sat beside me in our family pew. At the close of the service an after-meeting was held, John, with others, waited behind, and from John 3:16 was led to see God's rich provision in Jesus for his salvation. Three months before I had accepted Christ as my personal Saviour. Now we were one in the faith that is in Christ Jesus. Yes, and thank God, this oneness in spiritual fellowship was never broken throughout the twenty-six years of our Christian companionship. I well remember how my beloved father rejoiced when he realised that

God had answered his prayers in the conversion to Christ of his two boys, to be followed shortly after with the additional assurance that some of his daughters too had embraced Christ. Pray on, O ye saints of God, my father's God still lives, He can answer prayer as truly today as ever.

My brother's subsequent life story is largely told in this book by others, the further revelation and call he received in the year 1890, his going forth with whole-hearted zeal into his Lord's work in the village of Houston (his Jerusalem), and the surrounding villages. Suffice it, therefore, that I give only a few of the inner sidelights of his Christian character and work. In the course of time the Houston village mission, described so well on another page by Mr. Hugh Morris, came to an end. The mission, commenced by Mr. W.B. Sloan, in the summer of 1885, continued for some years. In the early nineties it was stopped. I was then from home in business, and only returned once every fortnight. My brother, with a few others, conducted open-air meetings every Sunday afternoon. When at home I gladly assisted. On one such occasion a big man who had repeatedly declared his intention of stopping these meetings, came upon the scene. Alas for us on this occasion, we numbered only two persons – my bother and myself. We sang a duet, then took our turn at preaching, The man would have none of it. He was six feet two or three inches in height, and powerfully built. He shook his fist in our faces, and threatened to deform us if we persisted in preaching, but my brother's indomitable spirit was in no way scared, we continued to preach and sing for Jesus, despite his threats. After a time he left us, and in peace we continued and concluded that somewhat eventful open-air meeting.

The work in the Gryffe Grove Hall, Bridge-of-Weir, and in Johnstone, and other neighbouring towns, with which my dear brother was so closely identified would require a volume by itself to do it justice. These were years of burning zeal for Christ and His Kingdom. Many were led to Christ through my brother's faithful gospel ministry, and God's people were quickened and revived. I had the unspeakable joy of assisting him, as opportunity afforded, in these early years and saw much of the inner side of his life, which was transparently clean and true. I gladly bear witness to this, I will not detail the story of how John was led to enter the Baptist ministry. This period in his life had three distinct chapters, viz., Govan, Paisley Road, Glasgow, and Walworth Road, London. In each sphere God's hand was distinctly laid upon His servant in power. But especially was this the case in Paisley Road, Glasgow. During his thirteen years' ministry there, hundreds upon hundreds were swept into Christ's Kingdom. Let me once more take you to the inner side of all this. Others will tell you the story from the outside. My beloved brother was a man mighty in prayer. He was a master in this holy art. In October, 1899, I came from Bradford, where I was then Pastor, to Paisley Road, to conduct a month's mission. Night after night, just as I was about to announce my text, John would slip off the platform into a small side vestry, and fall upon his knees in prayer. There he would wrestle with God, as I pled with men. Needless to say the results of that mission abide today. I have been with my dear brother in prayer, again and again, when his whole frame shook like an aspen leaf, so earnest was he in his pleadings with God for a perishing world. He often wept in prayer. Like his Lord he offered up his supplications with "strong crying and tears" (Heb. 5:7). Little wonder hard hearts were broken, and stubborn wills subdued under his ministry. As I listened to him in prayer I used to say, "Dear John is far ben." He seemed to live on the most intimate terms with his Lord. There was nothing mawkish about his piety. He never tried to make one feel that he was holier than others, yet one instinctively felt that he was a man of God, whose supreme joy was in fellowship with his Lord and Redeemer.

The full story of those thirteen years of consecrated Christian labour will never be told. To my beloved brother they were years of joy and sorrow. Every convert did not turn out to be a "crown of rejoicing" unto the Lord's servant. The weak and faltering ones caused my brother much pain, and backsliders nearly broke his heart. But the joys of this period more than counterbalanced its sorrows. Many sought and found Christ, and ever after followed on to know the Lord. It was during this time that two great sorrows befell my brother. In the summer of 1905 his health broke down, his voice, which was in the early days, rich and resonant, completely failed him. For six months he was unfit for duty. This was a very severe trial to him. He wept with me and I with him over this trial. However, a sea voyage and a complete rest, with special treatment, in due time brought back, at least, partial strength and energy to him. But he was never the same in physical fitness afterwards. Those who only knew him during his closing years saw but the skeleton of the former days, that is, in the physical power and mighty appeal. True, during the last five or six years of his life there was a wonderful mellowing, a ripening, that those of us who were in the more intimate fellowship did not fail to perceive. We saw the outer man waxing weaker, and the inner man stronger every time we met. But a greater sorrow still lay across his path. Mrs Harper was a real helpmeet to him. She was some years his senior, and was of a bright disposition. My brother and she, then Miss Bell, met during the Bridge-of-Weir mission work. For ten years they waited for each other. I greatly rejoiced in my brother's marriage with Miss Bell. But, alas! their married life was of short duration. It covered little more than two years. A little girl was born at New Year, 1906, and not many days later Mrs Harper's spirit "winged its flight to realms of day". I will never forget that event. I was then Pastor of Bellshill Baptist Church. It was Sunday evening, I had just given out my text, Isaiah 27:15 to 18 "A covenant with death," when I was called into the vestry, a policeman wanted to see me. He had received a message by wire from my brother. It read as follows, "Dear George, please come at once, Annie is dying. I want Mary and you beside me." The Mary here mentioned was my own wife. I returned to my service, called two of our office-bearers on to the platform, and left the service in their hands. A cab was hired, and with all speed my wife and myself got to my beloved brother's side in his deep sorrow. Ah, he was *my brother*, and nothing would have kept me from him in his trial. We stood by Mrs Harper's bed for twelve hours doing all in our power to comfort her, and alleviate her pain, and then, when her spirit entered the brighter home above, we gently closed her eyelids.

This trial, coming as it did upon the one through which he passed the year before, completely prostrated him. It was his Gethsemane, his fiery baptism. The cup was a bitter one, but he drank it, meanwhile saying, "Not my will, but Thine be done." Shortly after this, my dear wife prevailed upon him to allow us to keep wee Nana for him which he did for about six months. We would gladly have kept the little pet all through the year that followed for her father's sake, and for her own sake, but that joy was not granted us. My brother sadly missed the fellowship of his dear wife. His home was never the same to him after. He had a nature that craved for companionship. Only a few months before he was taken from us we were together for some days. It was like new life to him. We prayed, sang, walked, and talked much together. How he poured into my ear matters that touched his future, assuring me that to no other one had he thus opened his mind. Would that it had been God's will to have spared him to have carried through some of these plans and purposes.

When he accepted the invitation to the pastorate of the Church in Walworth Road, London, he wrote to me telling about his anticipated farewell services in Paisley Road. I was urgently requested by him to come to his farewell tea meeting. This I did ungrudgingly. I had been at his first induction service in Govan, and I sat, by his special request, at his side on this last occasion. What a meeting it was. Tears were shed and tributes paid to his sterling worth, but not one sentence in my hearing was exaggerated. In London, as in Glasgow, God set his seal on His servant's work. In one year the old Church, with many worthy traditions attached to its history, passed through a remarkable season of reviving grace. It bids fair, under the ministry of my esteemed friend and brother, Pastor A, Moncur Niblock, who was co-pastor with dear John, to rival Paisley Road. This was my conviction during a recent visit I paid to it. Then Chicago! Who can speak of the marvellous work accomplished through the instrumentality of my precious brother in the famous Moody Church in that city during the winter months of 1911-1912? Rev. E.Y. Woolley, assistant Pastor of that great Church, in a letter to me on 11th May, says, "I have returned to Chicago to find, as I expected, our people grief-stricken through the loss of Mr. Harper. Our mid-week meeting last night was crowded to the doors. We had fully three hundred more people than usually attend, and hundreds were weeping as the meagre details of his passing were told. I never knew a man who had so gripped the hearts of the people in three short months of fellowship. Next Sunday morning is to be given to a memorial service for him, but it is easy to see that every one of our meetings will be to a large extent memorials. God used him while here as I never have seen a man used before." Such is Mr. Woolley's testimony.

I possess a number of letters written to me by dear John from Chicago. The one vehement desire expressed in all these letters is that I would pray for him. "Pray for me, pray for me every minute," thus he wrote.

My brother never spared himself, but as the years advanced he seemed to sacrifice himself more and more for others, and specially for his Lord.

The Life of Faith, referring to this wonderful work of grace in Chicago, says, "His services were attended with such rich blessing that the visit lengthened into three months, the Moody Church passing through one of the most wonderful revivals in its history. The Lord's own people also received a spiritual uplift, a practical illustration of which was seen in the fact that a debt of £1,000 was wiped out in four days.

On his return from Chicago he paid a brief visit to Scotland, coming first to Edinburgh where he addressed two meetings, both being held in our Church at Gorgie. His word was with great power. From Edinburgh he travelled to Glasgow, then to Paisley, Denny, and Cumnock in Ayrshire. In all these places his ministry was "in the Holy Ghost and in much assurance," though he was considerably run down in body. At the urgent and most cordial request of the Moody Church in Chicago he consented to return for three months more. In a letter to me dated London, 1st April, he wrote, "We are sailing on Saturday with the *Lusitania* from Liverpool." Would God he had gone by that boat instead of the ill-fated *Titanic* a week later. The *Titanic* sailed from Southampton for New York on 10th of April. On the 15th of April she went down into the bosom of the ocean, carrying with her 1503 precious lives, and amongst these my own beloved brother and companion, John Harper. The details of this sad disaster need not be re-told by me here; they are known to everybody, I suppose, in our land, more or less, and I daresay the generation after the present one will be familiar with this dreadful catastrophe at sea, in calm weather, when the acme of man's genius in mercantile shipbuilding on her maiden voyage perished. I cannot attempt to explain the Providence that removes such a man of God in the midst of his usefulness. I can only say my confidence is in the over-ruling wisdom of God. "Some day we'll understand." I think Keble puts it well when he writes:

"Thy God hath said 'tis good for thee
To walk by faith and not by sight,
Take it on trust a little while;
Soon shalt thou read the mystery right,
In the bright sunshine of His smile."

One truly feels this is all one can do in the presence of such a Providence. There was no farewell message sent to us from the sinking ship, not even a parting kiss, so far as we know, given to his little child. Calm and collected he handed her to one of the ship's officials on the top deck, whilst he himself remained by others of the captain on the second deck. This was only half an hour before the mighty leviathan took her final plunge. What his thoughts were during that last half hour on earth, no one will ever tell. One thing we rest assured of, there was, "no moaning at the bar" when he "put out to sea." He was "the abundant entrance."

"E'en for the dead, I will not bind my soul to grief,
As though death can divide:
For is it not as though the rose that claimed my garden wall,
Had blossomed on the other side?
Death doth hide
But not divide –
Thou art but on the other side,
Thou art with Christ and Christ with me,
In Christ united still are we."

Along with scores of others an esteemed brother writes to me, "Do not grudge the liberty your Heavenly Father has taken with you. He has honoured you, and at the same time fulfilled his own promise, 'where I am there shall also my servant be.' The angels would have a warm welcome for your brother. Think more of the life that is, than of the life that was. More of the abundant entrance, than of the strange, sudden departure. Love and wisdom are on the throne – perfect love and perfect wisdom. It may seem at times all so strange, but it must be right. Try and dig a well in your Valley of Baca." Thanks, dear brother, this is what I have been trying to do, and as my well becomes deeper, my soul longs yet more and more for the glorious coming morn when the enigmas of life will be read in "His light clearly".

I would like to say here how deeply I value all the kind messages of sympathy that I have received in this my hour of sorrow and weeping. Will friends please accept of this assurance of my personal appreciation? I am not alone in my sorrow. My dear wife has been broken-hearted over the loss of her brother-in-law. Then my sisters – Mrs Sinclair and Mrs Given in Johnstone, Mrs Balloch in St. Boswell's, and Mrs Auckland in Govan, all weep with me over our irreparable loss. Our brother was very dear to us as a family. To one and all of us his "love was wonderful," and by his (sisters and brother) it was reciprocated. His little girl, Nana, does not realise her great loss yet. May her father's God put his mantle over her and protect her from the blast of a cold, sinful world! May our Heavenly Father's will concerning her be carried out, and in some measure at least, her earthly father's spirit of devotion to his Lord in due time be found in her.

Multitudes sorrow over the loss of my beloved brother. He was a great soul-winner, and a true pastor. He led multitudes to the feet of Christ, and afterwards fed them upon the finest of wheat. His analytic and homiletic gifts were of a very high order, as will be seen in another part of this book, and as other brethren gladly bear witness to this fact I merely mention it. However, the following illustration will not be out of place here. Text, Galatians 2:20. 1st, we have here the grand conception of the Gospel, "I am crucified with Christ". 2nd, we have here the grand condition of the Gospel, "Nevertheless I live." 3rd, we have here the grand confession of the Gospel, "Yet not I, but Christ," etc., etc.

This method of "rightly dividing the Word of Truth" commended itself to the vast majority of my brother's hearers. You will notice this message was one which was meant to gather the minds of his audience around the Cross. This was ever his object, "Christ, only Christ." In a letter to one of his sisters, as far back as 27th of June, 1892, when he was a young preacher, he wrote, "Oh that we could only have more faith in a loving, living Saviour, and that we would only open our hearts wide enough to receive more of His sweet, consuming, constraining, heart-piercing love, and oh! that we would open our ears to hear the sweet voice of the Bridegroom as He whispers to our souls, 'Arise, my love, my fair one, and come away, and leave the fleeting phantoms of this fleeting day.' And oh, that His soul-ravishing voice would so reach our cold hearts that we would be made to thirst and cry out for a closer fellowship with the crucified Saviour." Such is only a brief quotation from a letter in front of me, many parts of which one feels are too sacred for public print. Ah, yes! the message of the Cross was the message of his burning ministry from first to last. But perhaps in a very special degree the Cross filled his vision during his closing ministry. His intention was to write and publish in book form some of these addresses which God used in the Chicago movement, but God saw fit to write them in another way, indelibly upon the hearts and lives of ransomed sinners and revived saints. Some hundreds of his rich and suggestive outlines are buried in an ocean grave.

Nevertheless of his witness and work for his Lord we can truly say, "He being dead yet speaketh."

There was a side of my brother's character which seemed somewhat out of harmony with the side I have written at length upon. He was very easily imposed upon. I often remonstrated with him regarding this. I could easily give instance after instance from my own personal knowledge of how he suffered, and sometimes severely and for long, at the hands of those who were little short of impostors. But he would only reply when remonstrated with, "Well, well, the Lord knows about them, He will deal with them." But for this little weakness in his character, to some of us who knew him intimately, he would have been little short of our ideal in human perfection. The reader will please be assured that I seek in all I write concerning my beloved brother to magnify the grace of Christ as so wonderfully manifested in His servant. It was the grace of Christ that saved him, sanctified him, and now has glorified him in the presence of his Lord and Redeemer in the Paradise of God. It was that same grace operating within his heart that gave to him such a boundless passion for the salvation of the lost, and at one and the same time wrought in him such deep devotion to the Person and work of Christ. May this passion more and more be mine! I feel this poor, groaning, dying world, steeped in sin, and openly rejecting Christ, can ill afford to part with a man of God like my brother, who constantly wept over it, and poured out his life's strength for it. I also feel the Church of Christ, alas, so often lethargic, can ill afford to bid adieu to a ministry so awakening, so needful. But it may be God in this way is calling to deeper consecration, to truer service, to the filling of the breach made by dear John's translation, some others of His servants, "Whilst Thou'rt calling, Lord, call me." May multitudes be baptised with the same spirit and zeal and enthusiasm for the glory of Christ, the conversion of the lost, and the hastening of the day of the long looked-for coming of our Lord and Saviour Jesus Christ.

"If we but knew that through the closing door
Some one we love would never enter more,
Would we not hasten without richest store?
If we but knew!

If we but knew that from the market-place,
Soon we would miss some kind familiar face,
Would our cold greetings not be touched with grace?
If we but knew!

If we but knew some heart beside our own,
Had walked in darkest Gethsemane alone,
Oh, with what largeness would our love be shown?
If we but knew!

Dear Jesus, patient, understanding, kind,
We are Thy lost sheep in a winter wind,
Forgive us that we are so wilful blind!
Teach us to know!"

5

A Man of Vision

Tribute - Pastor John Dick

To write an appreciation of John Harper is no easy task; for when one has written in the superlative degree, one feels that justice has not been done to the life-work and character of this strenuous worker for God. I knew Mr. Harper for twelve years, and seven years ago, I spent ten days with him while conducting a special mission in Paisley Road. Then I learned to love him, and to know John Harper better was to love him more. We were different men, but there was an affinity between us that strengthened with the years, and his great desire was that I should succeed him in Paisley Road, if ever he should be led out of it. That is now an accomplishment fact; but little did we think that his earthly race would be completed at thirty-nine. In losing our dear brother, we have lost a great preacher. Stepping out from the ranks of the working men, he stood before his fellows as a man taught of God. No college can claim him; he came forth a preacher from God. The passion of his life was soul-winning. It was no unusual thing for him never to go to bed on a Saturday night, pleading for souls, and crying for Divine Power to enable him to preach for the glory of God. It was this passionate love for souls that made him literally live among the people. With pride the people of the district tell me how he used to drop in to dinner or tea, and sit down with them to their frugal meal, served on a table devoid of cloth. He was one of themselves, losing himself in their sorrows and joys – advising and warning, rejoicing and weeping – and in this manly, loving way he endeared himself to the simple people who today mourn his loss as if he had been one of their own family. His love and sympathy were phenomenal, because of the magnetic sympathetic influence that ever emanated from him. No wonder Roman Catholic and Protestant, the poor and the poorest of the poor, shed copious tears at the mention of his death! The district loved him and appreciated the herculean efforts of this great, passionate worker for God. He was a great Bible student, and his capable teaching is manifest in the numbers of young men in the congregation who have an intelligent grasp of the Book of Books, and who have caught Pastor Harper's enthusiasm for Bible study. In Paisley Road and Walworth Road, London, his magnificent grasp of Bible truths was instrumental in bringing back many to the main line who had gone off to side tracks. One man in a prominent position in London told the writer that he owed his present position to John Harper who had convinced him of doctrinal error by his intelligent exposition of the Living Word. Another prominent worker for God says, that but for John Harper he would today have been wandering in the mazes of infidelity.

Reclaimed drunkards, gamblers, prize fighters, now enthusiastic workers for God, all praise the Saviour whom they love for the day they came into touch with John Harper. Personal dealing was his great forte, his tact and greatness of soul eminently fitting him for this work. He knew working-men's difficulties and temptations; he knew their literature and their manner of thinking; because he was one of them, and while some of them might resent what they called his *extreme attitude*, yet they loved him and were the first to recognise his intense sincerity.

He was a great open-air preacher, and could always command large and appreciative audiences People speak with pride of the effect of his magnificent voice in the open-air, and tell how cleverly and firmly he could deal with all kinds of interruptions. No one could "floor" him, his great and intelligent grasp of Bible truths enabling him to successfully combat all assailants. It was a very common sight to see souls being dealt with in the open-air, some even kneeling down in the ring and making confession of sin. Some of these trophies of grace are today deacons and respected members of Paisley Road Baptist Church, which is built on the spot where many of its members once gambled and fought! What a testimony to the power of the Gospel, working through a man completely abandoned to the great work of soul-winning!

What a sermon builder he was! His homiletical ability was marvellous. His great doctrinal sermons grew under his treatment until they appeared like a magnificent branching tree, affording shade and shelter to many a weary traveller. His wide knowledge of Puritan, Theological and Revival literature enabled him to embellish his discourses in such a way as to send the hearer away with a sense of satisfaction and fullness. How difficult it is for one to realise that this great, intelligent, earnest, enthusiastic preacher and soul winner has gone out of one's life! All denominations mourn his loss, for his energies were freely given to all, as he didn't know the meaning of ministerial jealousy. His life will be an inspiration to thousands, his influence will be indelible, his example infectious, and although he was struck down in the zenith of his usefulness, yet we do not grudge him his translation to higher service. To try to fill his place is to attempt the impossible, yet to *be in his place* is an inspiration.

He has gone to his reward, and it is for those who knew and loved him to profit by his example and try to fill the gap as far as is possible.

Farewell, my beloved brother! May your mantle as a preacher, fall upon your unworthy successor, and may the passion that filled your soul control the writer of this inadequate appreciation.

6

A Man of Passion

Tribute - Pastor Hugh Gunn

Our dear brother, Mr. Harper, was: 1. A man in Christ.He was wholly surrendered to God, I knew him well, and I never saw in him anything to the contrary. He had no hobby, and sought no recreation other than the deepening of his delight in God. Every power and passion of his being seemed to thrill with the life of God. He was on the altar continually. 2, He was a man of intense earnestness. This earnestness was begotten of his consciousness of God. The power of the world to come seemed to rest on him at all times. This characterized him continually, whether praying, preaching, or dealing personally with individuals regarding salvation. 3, He was a man of prayer. I shall never forget seasons of prayer with him. He no sooner began praying audibly than every one felt he was in touch with God. After hearing him pray, one felt the desire to go away alone and open out one's heart before God. Prayer took a great deal out of him. He laboured in prayer, praying in the Holy Ghost. It was quite a common thing for him to spend whole nights alone in prayer. He literally came from the presence of God to his people. His sermons were saturated with prayer. Hence their great power in uplifting and sanctifying God's people, and bringing sinners weeping to the Cross. 4, He was a man of God. A holy man of God. God was all in all to him. He was always in communion with God. He revealed in the preciousness of Christ. God's hand of power rested upon him. This undoubtedly was the secret of his constant possession of that indescribable, undefinable thing we call unction. I never heard him speak without it.

II. As a Pastor. 1, He was most careful in his preparation for the pulpit, He reminded one of McCheyne's saying, "beaten oil for the sanctuary." Saint and sinner seemed to be thoroughly understood by him, and each had their portion dealt out to them as in the sight of God. With what eagerness he sought to lead God's people into the fullness of the blessed life in Christ, dreading their remaining satisfied with anything short of the abundant, overflowing life which filled his own soul. He was greatly blessed in leading Christians out into the service of Christ. He never urged them to be or to do that which he was not or did. He led the way. 2, Our beloved brother possessed a consuming zeal for souls. This was really the outstanding feature of his consecrated life. He seemed to be unable to live without souls being won to Christ. Souls! Souls!! Souls!!! coloured his whole life. 3, He was loyal to God's Word. He never descended into the questionable paths of higher criticism. To him it was God's Word. 4, He was most intolerant with regard to some of the modern methods of doing Christian work. To him it was little short of blasphemy to offer dying men entertainments and amusements instead of the glorious Gospel which bringeth salvation to all men. His own work was a living example of what the Gospel alone can accomplish.

III. His End. Being greatly blessed to the Moody Church, Chicago, he was invited to return for a second mission, and on his way there Christ came to him and said, "Come up higher." What a meeting with his Lord! I am intensely curious to know how he acted in the closing moments of his life. Would he not, as was his wont, be drying the tear away, comforting, and helping till the last moment of his life? Would he not in the midst of that sweltering mass of drowning men, women and children be pointing them to the Cross, and thus as he lived, die with that one name upon his lips – Jesus! Jesus!! Jesus!!!?

7

A Man of Mission

Tribute - Pastor A M Niblock

It is with indescribable feeling that I stand here this morning. The great calamity which has fallen upon us, in the loss of our beloved pastor, the Rev. John Harper, has plunged us into a pathless darkness from which for the moment our hearts and minds cannot find a way out. Last Monday evening we went from the prayer meeting to our homes full of praise to God for the preservation of our beloved friend. The newspapers told us he was upon an unsinkable ship, that all was safe, and therefore there was no need to fear, but alas! man's word is not like God's word – immutable, unchanging and sure. Neither are man's works like God's, for both words and works have failed, as has been seen in this sad disaster. The ship was sinkable and she sank, and with her went down into the dark deep the body of him whom we loved so well, but, praise God, we know he himself has gone home to be with the Lord.

We have suffered a great loss, and not only we, but the entire Church of God, a loss which cannot be replaced. There was only one John Harper, and there will never be another, no one will ever fill his place. He has gone; we are left, left! For what? To weep and allow our hands to hang down? No, surely no! but to work, to watch, to wait, to preach

Christ and Him crucified, and thus to save those who are crying out to us , "Save our souls."

My heart sympathises with yours, yes, we are suffering together, and God only knows the extent of the void that is in your hearts this morning.

You have lost a friend, a brother, a leader and a pastor. Words of mine cannot comfort you, but I do lovingly offer you the comfort wherewith I have been comforted, and which is, that I know "He is with Christ, which is far better," "that I shall see him again." Therefore, I would turn you to Him who has been sent to the world for this purpose, even the Holy Ghost. He will be your Comforter if you will let Him. He will guide you into the truth of this disaster. He will explain the silence of God, and still every suggestion that would cause you to rebel against this dispensation which has been allowed to come upon us. Let us not forget the Word of God which says, "Casting all your care upon Him, for He careth for you" (I Peter 5:7). He knows the way to take, and although we seem to be in a dark, pathless wilderness, dazed and stunned, He will lead us gently out into the comforting shade of His own presence, which we so much need at this present time.

God loves this Church. He honoured it by giving for a season, this man of prayer, to lead it into the green pastures of truth, and to the quiet waters of communion with God. The very fact that he was found here proves the love of God for you, and that God has chosen this people for Himself, that He might show forth His glory and virtue through you. Today you are in the furnace of affliction. But is that not when God chooses His people? Isaiah says, "I have chosen you in the furnace of affliction," and so in this which has come upon us, God is choosing us for Himself.

Is God testing us, as He tested the followers of Gideon? Is He watching to see how we shall stoop and drink? Testing us to see how we shall act, how we shall conduct ourselves? Oh, may the fire consume the dross, and leave nothing but pure gold, as it did with Job. Dear Samuel Rutherfold in a letter to a mother who had lost a child, wrote, "You might indeed be cast down if you were alone in the furnace; but He who went through Gethsemane is with you, and He will take you through; that soft, sweet hand of His will lead you out again into the land of peace and rest."

At such a time as this our practice must harmonise with our preaching, and we must follow the example of our Master and also our dear brother in remembering others. England today is a land of mourning. There are many widows and orphans who, but a short time ago were counting the days, yea hours, when they would have the joy of meeting their loved ones again. Today their hearts are crushed. Desolation has entered into their spirits, and they are lonely, their future is dark, and the spirit of the companionless has taken hold of them. Now they have no one to lean upon, to look up to, to commune with, their partner has gone, that one who was their other being, that one in whom they had lost themselves, and of whom they themselves were a part.

God help us then to play the part of the true Christian and remember these in our prayers, before the eternal throne. I have said that we have lost a friend, a brother and a pastor. This is true, is it not? He was a friend indeed. We could go to him and open our hearts, knowing that he would hold sacred our confidence, that he would be gentle with us, and deal with us tenderly and that whatever advice he gave could be relied upon.

He was a brother. His ways were brotherly, there was no stand-off, superior-sort-of-spirit with him. He was reachable, you felt he was one with you, you were of the same blood, the same family, he truly fraternized with you. In other words you felt he was your own. Your burdens were his burdens, your sorrows his sorrows, your joys his joys. He entered into your life – in as much as you would allow him – and made you feel that he would stand by you through thick and thin. Then he was a pastor, a shepherd. It was borne in upon you that he was a man who realized that he had to render an account to the great Shepherd of the flock over which he had the oversight.

He fed you. He didn't ask you what kind of food you liked or what you thought you wanted, for he knew what was good for you. Sometimes it was sweet, tender grass, sometimes bitter herbs, sometimes he had to use the rod, but oh, how lovingly he did it.

He prayed for you. How he prayed! Some few of us had the privilege of spending seasons together with him in waiting upon God, and at these times he would lose himself entirely, often have we been amazed at his boldness, asking God for great things, and speaking to Him as if he were well acquainted with him. I have never met any man who was his equal in wrestling with God. I have seen the sweat literally pour from him as he agonized in prayer. At times he seemed to have taken eagle wings to himself and be far away from us, far away in that blue sky where God is, and yet at the same time we realized that he brought heaven down to earth. When John Harper prayed heaven and earth met, and those near him knew it, because they felt it. He was a Brainerd, an Edwards, a McCheyne, a William Burns, a Finney, and a Caughey rolled into one. How he prayed for the lambs of the flock! O friends, we owe a great debt to our Lord Jesus for allowing him to enter into our life. We are spiritually richer today because of his prayers, and in days to come when spiritual blessings fall upon us, remember that in a great measure many of them will be the answers to our departed brother's prayers.

Our friend, brother, and pastor has gone home. When his dear wife was taken from him some six years ago, he was, in a new sense, a homeless man. It was his wife that made that home, just a little outside Glasgow, "home" to him. Now he has gone to her, and yet far better than even this, he has gone to his Lord and Saviour, whom he adored, loved and served.

When the *Titanic* went down it took with it his poor frail body, but not his spirit, for that has gone home to God. We must not, therefore, think of him as we knew him after the flesh, but as he is now with Christ. If we think of the man after the flesh, we shall see the poor body down in the sea, and imagine that he is cold and lonely, which is not so. No, friends, we sorrow not as others. That body was but the earthly dwelling place of a noble man of God. The man has gone, and the earthly tabernacle is now tenantless. We would if we could, cover and guard, and lovingly lay that body in the grave, because of the soul that once lived in it, but we cannot, and we, therefore, submit and bow to the will of God. For God has been pleased to take our brother to Himself in this manner, for what purpose we do not know, but one thing we do know, *God has done right*, and to His will we say, Amen!

8

A Man among Men

His peers commended John Harper
Tribute - Pastor M Ferguson, Anniesland

It was my privilege and joy to know the late Pastor John Harper for over twelve years. I first heard of him at New Cumnock, where he had been holding some meetings. The church formed there by Mr. James Adair was looking out for a pastor and were very keen to secure Mr. Harper. I saw the fruits of his mission, and felt any church would be justified in securing such a man of God.

I afterwards met him in the Gordon Halls, Paisley Road, and when I saw the spirit and enthusiasm of the meetings, I said to one of the workers, "You won't keep Mr. Harper long here."

Well, he was not to be so easily lifted out of Paisley Road. He found his sphere there for many years, and hundreds will thank God through all eternity for his faithful ministry in that place. Others will tell the tale of the church, its enlargement, its constant revivals, the overflowing crowds, and the hundreds of souls saved and blessed.

I was often there during 1905, when the news of the Welsh Revival spread. I did not go to Wales, but often saw scenes in Paisley Road Church similar to what we heard were going on there. The crowds were so great it was difficult to get in, and after getting in, still more difficult to get near the platform. Then, before any one could speak ten minutes, souls were crying out for mercy under the mighty power of God. It was not excitement. It was the Holy Spirit convicting of sin. One was forced to ask often, What is the secret of this perennial blessing in Paisley Road? But when in touch with the Pastor in his vestry or in his home, the secret was soon found out.

Nobody could be in Mr. Harper's presence long till it was found what a mighty man of God he was, especially in prayer. He knew God. He knew his Bible, and he knew by heart-felt experience the indwelling power of the Holy Spirit. He had a passionate love for Christ and souls. It often amazed me the amount of work Mr. Harper went through. When he studied, and how he prepared the marvelous addresses he gave, was a wonder to many. But when most of us were sleeping he was in the secret place of the Most High, closeted with God and His Word all night in the little room off the vestry in Paisley Road Church.

After Mrs. Harper's death he would often stay overnight in the church and pray for the occupants of every seat, and then on Sabbath he would look for and expect souls to be saved. He was a burning and a shining light. Some burn and don't shine; others shine but don't burn. When he spoke it might be said what was said by the man who went to hear Rowland Hill, "The words come hissing hot from his heart." He believed what he preached, and preached what he believed. Christ and eternal things were all so real to him. He lived and preached "as if Christ died yesterday, rose today, and was coming tomorrow."

If ever a preacher was conscious of the presence of God it was Mr. Harper, and he made his hearers feel the same. I once heard him say at a conference, "We won't get many sinners convicted and converted through laughs and jokes. Some have laughed the Spirit of God out of Gospel meetings, and the one thing we are conscious of above all others in many meetings, is the lack of the deep sense of the presence and power of God."

Mr. Harper was also a born expositor. On one occasion he was with us helping in a tent mission. It was Friday night, and we were comparing notes for the coming Sabbath. "What is your morning message?' he asked at the supper table. "Job 29:2 is the text," I answered. Knowing his marvellous gift and mastery of the art of homiletics, I said, "Now let me hear your divisions. How would you handle it?" The subject dropped at the table, and no more was said till we got to the station at 10.45. "Oh," he said, "we forgot about the text, but I will look it up on the way home." The first post on Saturday brought me the following outline, with details, on a post card:- Text, "Oh that I were as in months past." 1st A humble remembrance of past blessings. 2nd A bitter regret for present barrenness. 3rd A sincere request for speedy restoration.

Alas! we shall compare no more notes down here, and we say of him what Jonathan said of David: "You will be missed for your place will be vacant." How some of us miss him! His cheery word, his helpful message, and above all the inspiration of his magnetic presence. I never left his company but I came home to pray. This was invariably the effect Mr. Harper's presence had on me. May a double portion of his holy, consecrated spirit fall on those of us who are left a little while longer, not only to "Hold the fort," but to storm the forts of darkness as our brother loved to do.

Tribute - Mr Hugh Morris, Evangelist

It was my privilege to have the friendship of Mr. John Harper for twenty-five years, and on reading the news of his sad end from the newspapers, after the awful *Titanic* disaster, could scarcely credit that such could be the fate of one I had parted with but a short time before, who, never since I had known him, seemed more fit for work physically, intellectually and spiritually. I had heard him preach frequently, but the address he gave at the Noon Meeting in Bothwell Street, Glasgow, on the day of our last meeting on earth, Wednesday, 20th March, stamped itself upon my mind by its lucidity, earnestness and spiritual power, making one feel sure that his gifts as a proclaimer of God's good news were not spent, but had increased and strengthened since I had previously been in his company.

Twenty-five years ago he began as a boy of fully fourteen years to work in the gardens of Barrochan House, Houston, Renfrewshire. Of sallow complexion and fragile frame, he did not look very strong. No one could have anticipated that he would have lived through those years to perform the great work he did, for as a worker in the Master's vineyard he laboured incessantly, as all know who came into contact with him. One marked feature of those early years that made radiant his young life was his reverence for the things of God. One year before our coming together, Mr. Walter Sloan, now of the China Inland Mission, conducted Gospel meetings in the village of Houston, when a good work was done. At that time he was brought to a saving knowledge of Jesus as his Saviour. After those meetings regular work was carried on, consisting of Sabbath morning meetings and meetings on Sabbath and Thursday nights. I have seen few villages in my time where, throughout the year, workers were more earnest, constant and warmhearted in lifting up the Saviour, and I do not think I am overstating the case when I say that for good attendance at all the meetings all the year round, none within my ken has eclipsed them. John was a regular attender and this no doubt proved helpful in bringing him on in his Christian life. He also attended the Free Church regularly, and heard many a good sermon from the Rev. George Lang. All this was no doubt conductive to the upbuilding of young John Harper. But it was my good fortune to know John's parents, and who can over-estimate the benign influence of a home where Christ is Lord and Master, upon the young life growing up in the midst? His father was a most unassuming man, yet withal a man who made himself felt, for the love of God that filled his heart made him think, speak and act in such a manner as to declare with no uncertain voice that he was a "servant of Jesus Christ" as the following incident will show. One day in a farmyard, the workers were putting up hay in stacks, the farmer, started to taunt him and sneer at his religion as he passed by. The workers laughed. George Harper said nothing for a time, but afterwards turning on him he repeated Rev. 21:8, and some other texts of a kindred nature. The laughter ceased, the old farmer stood trembling, then turning on his heel fled into the house. From that day on no one of that farm ever attempted to make light of George Harper or his religion. A man of true piety, mighty in the Scripture and powerful in prayer. Many a day at the meal hour I have sat with my Bible in hand and listened with great profit to this "Master in Israel" opening up the Scripture. No one could listen to him as he prayed and not be moved by the melting earnestness and intensity of the man. One could never doubt but that he knew the straight road to the throne of grace. I write this to show that John Harper had the great advantage of a truly Christian home, and that pious parents, though obscure from the eye of the great outside world, may plant and nurture little spiritual acorns that may grow up to be great spiritual oaks, "trees, the planting of the Lord."

I had left that district and gone home to reside at Largs. John Harper had gone to work in the carpet work at Elderslie, later on in the paper mill at Kilbarchan. The call came to preach the Gospel, and he obeyed. All round that district, Johnstone, Kilbarchan, Linwood, Elderslie, and Bridge-of-Weir he went preaching with power. First the School House and then a hall was taken for meetings in Bridge-of-Weir. I was asked several times to spend a weekend there. One meeting lives in my memory. The Sabbath day was wet and stormy. At the hour of meeting at night the weather had not improved. We were looking for a small gathering, as the way leading to the hall was down a long, dark, somewhat circuitous lane lined with trees. When on the platform, after he had given out the hymn, I asked him if he thought there were any unsaved present. He knew the workers well, and after a minute he whispered to me, "There are five here who have not yet decided for Christ." I asked him to pray for the conversion of these five, and I would preach for their conversation. "Agreed," he said, with a smile. When the first meeting was over no one made to go away. No pressure was brought to bear upon any, nor stratagems used to trap them. All voluntarily sat still, and on the five being asked if they desired to trust Christ they said they did, and all five made profession of faith in Jesus before leaving the hall. He used to speak of this meeting when we met in after days.

Another gathering he organized was an open-air conference for Christian workers on the Brae of Ranfurly, Bridge-of-Weir, on a Saturday afternoon in the summer time. I took part in giving an address at that conference, and can remember still the large gathering and the healthy spiritual life displayed by all present. When one calls to mind that at this time he was not quite 20 years of age, and yet the leading spirit in all this work, it shows us that, coupled with those succeeding years of arduous toil and unfading zeal for the winning of the lost for Christ, he was not labouring in energy of the flesh, but in the "power of the spirit," having received orders from "the Leader and Commander" to go forth.

Of him it can be said now that his day's work is over, having put "his hand to the plough" he never looked back. About the time when he was carrying on work in full swing in the above mentioned district, he wrote to me saying he saw, and was convinced from the Word of God that he should be baptized by immersion, also requesting me to perform the rite. I was not a pastor, nor at that time had even the title of "evangelist," but as he was insistent that I should baptize him, one Sabbath morning we went together to the Noodle Burn on the north side of Largs, and there, in the pool under the bridge on the Wemyss Bay Road, John Harper, in obedience to his Lord, was baptized in New Testament form.

The last time I saw his godly father in life we had a talk together of the "things concerning the King." And though at that time he was going about following his daily occupation, most calmly and with emphasis he assured me that he knew he was near the end of his sojourn here. In health, he was his usual, but he told me the prayers of many years had been answered, and the home call would come soon. True it was, for ere two weeks had passed I was in Houston at his funeral.
Towards the end of last March I shook hands with John. He was going off shortly afterwards to Chicago. He said, "I may see you out there yet." "Yes, keep believing," was my rejoinder. No. Not Chicago, but "the City which hath foundation," where no Gospel campaigns are carried on, no sin, no partings, no heart-rending catastrophes, no blinding griefs. With Christ, with Him for ever, we shall meet, bless God.

O Thou great and kind Shepherd of the flock of God, take charge of the tender lamb that has been left behind, lead her along the sheltered side of life's road, and bring her to Thy glory, and to her mother and to her father at the hour of daybreak. Amen.

Tribute - Mr W D Dunn, Evangelist

I gladly contribute my affectionate testimony to the fidelity and sterling worth of the late Pastor John Harper. I knew him for over twenty years, and during all that period we were in the closest fellowship with each other, in seeking the sanctification of the saints of God, and the salvation of perishing souls. During my long experience in Christian work I have been in touch with the cream of the Lord's dear workmen, and without reserve, I can say that no pastor, nor teacher, nor evangelist ever moved my inner being more than the pleading and preaching of Pastor John Harper did; as he was always on flame for God and souls.

John Welch, in the corner of his glebe, at the midnight hour, said, "Oh God, give me Scotland, or I die;" and how often I have heard Pastor Harper say, when lying on his face before God, covered with perspiration, "Oh God, give me souls, or I die." Then he would sob and weep, as if his heart would break. Can we wonder that God gave him souls for Christ, in hundreds?

Our beloved brother was a deep student of the precious Word of God – he believed it was God-breathed from Genesis to Revelation; and he preached it with a clear vision.

I have often seen his after-meetings in Paisley Road Baptist Church more like a battlefield than anything else; saints sobbing on account of their unlikeness to Christ, and poor lost sinners crying out for salvation.

What glorious triumphs of grace were won through his Holy Ghost ministry in that part of the city! And wherever he went, whether in public or in private, he carried with him the holy fragrance of his Lord. I often felt, after being with him in the Gospel or at our

Royal Lord's Court, that he was fast ripening for higher service. He lived next door to heaven, hence his soul was constantly inhaling heaven's atmosphere. The blessing of soul our brother enjoyed saved him from every vestige of sectarianism; so that he preached in perfect harmony with all the other sections of the Christian Church. He had learned through grace that the Church and the work of the Church are one, and he was ready to lend a helping hand to any brother minister who desired his services. Many of us wondered how he lived under the tremendous strain, occasioned by the amount of preaching he went through, and the nights he spent in prayer, which seemed enough to kill the strongest of men; but on he went like an express train, determined to reach its destination without hindrance; his eyes steadily fixed upon his crucified, buried, risen, ascended, pleading and coming Lord. And all the powers of hell could not move him from his soul's centre.

And now the brave soldier's precious form lies beneath the ocean waves, and his blood-washed spirit is present with the Lord in yon land of light and glory, the homeland of all who love and serve the Christ of God.

"Oh what a home! Love upon Love
Re-echoing through its breadth;
The Son's divine affections flow
Throughout its height and depth.
And full response the Father gives,
Heart answering to heart,
And not a cloud to cross the scene
A shadow to impart.

"Oh what a home! But such His love
That He must fetch us there,
To fill that home, to be with Him,
And all His glory share,
The Father's house, the Father's heart,
All that the Son is given
Made ours – the object of His love –
And He, our joy of heaven."

Farewell, beloved soldier, we shall meet you in the morning without a cloud.

Tribute - Mr John Patton, Evangelist, Carmyle

I am thankful to have the opportunity of putting on record how much I owe in my Christian life to friendship with dear John Harper. I have found the word of Proverbs 17:27 to be true indeed, and the two friends now with the Lord who had most to do with the "sharpening" of my life were Matthew Colquhoun and John Harper.

Both were close friends, not only of my own, but of each other, and oftentimes before he fell on sleep on 6th May, 1909, Matthew served the Lord at Paisley Road during John Harper's pastorate. The one impressed me tremendously by the sweet and transparent holiness of his life, the other no less by his burning and devoted zeal, both qualities being manifestly born of their ardent love to the Saviour. When one experiences how easy it is to allow the keen edge of spiritual life to dull, one prizes the privilege of such friendships as these, and how many of the rank and file of our Christian Community, like myself, must have been blessed through contact with these two lives, eternity alone will reveal. To be in the company of John Harper was to have created anew in one's heart the desire to "spend and be spent" in the Master's service. Some of us can well imagine him in these last awful minutes on board the doomed *Titanic*, standing amidst a group of stricken, repentant souls pointing them to the Saviour he had loved and served so well and helping them seize their eleventh-hour opportunity. God has not many servants whom He could trust with such a service, and that to me at least is the explanation of our brother being on board the *Titanic* instead of the *Lusitania* as he had at one time planned.

May we all follow John Harper in so far as he followed Jesus.

9

A Man of God

His peers commended John Harper
Tribute - Mr Wm R Andrew

It is hard to realise that the friend and brother who was so much to us has been removed from this scene of labour, and that we shall never again here join heart and hand with him in proclaiming the love of Jesus to this poor sin-stricken world. Yet it is true. He has gone to higher service, called up higher by his Lord, whom he so truly loved and followed. What joy must be our dear brother's now as he gazes upon the face of Jesus – upon the One who even here had ravished his heart with His love.

I first met Mr. Harper nearly fourteen years ago, shortly after the commencement of his ministry in the Gordon Halls, Paisley Road. Since then it was my privilege and joy to be with him from time to time, sometimes in Paisley Road Church, and sometimes in other parts of Scotland, labouring in the service of the Master. After each of these seasons of fellowship, whether short or more protracted, the impression received at the first meeting was deepened and strengthened. Here was a man who knew God, and one who knew how to reach God in prayer!

After Mr. Harper left Glasgow for London it was my great delight to join him on several occasions in the work of publishing in that great city and in Wales, the old Gospel story of Jesus and His Love.

When he requested me by cable to proceed to Chicago, an immediate departure was arranged, and I reached him in the first week in December last. The fight had been strenuous, and though it had been followed by sweeping victory, our brother was tired and not over-well. He expressed satisfaction at the "sicht of a weel-kent face frae Bonnie Scotland," and he seemed comforted. He was doing his work in his usual style – morning prayer meeting at six o'clock, another prayer meeting at noon, Bible reading in the afternoon, and public meeting in the evening. The gaps between the meetings were filled up with interviews, visits, funerals, and attempts to meet the other innumerable demands that were made upon his time. Throughout the entire visit the fact that God's Holy Spirit was undoubtedly at work was easily discernible. Deep conviction of sin, confession, restitution on the part of many, conflict with those of God's people who were compromising with the world, warfare with principalities and power and spiritual hosts of darkness – these were the evidences in these meetings of His working.

The preaching of our brother was in demonstration of the Spirit and of power. His themes were the Cross of Christ, God's marvellous grace to man, the soon coming of our Lord Jesus Christ. His messages on grace held his audiences spell-bound by the hour. As the Spirit of God carried the truth home to the hearts of his hearers, he called upon them to yield, repeating over and over again the words of a favourite chorus:

"Nay, but I yield, I yield, I can hold out no more.
I sink, by dying love constrained, and own Thee conqueror."

The message of Galatians 2:20 was another upon which our dear brother laid great emphasis. Often he would have the audience repeat the words of that text carefully and prayerfully, and, as they did so, many entered into a new conception of its meaning, and a new experience of its truth by accepting "God's reckoning alone." The following words of a hymn were many times upon his own lips:

> "Buried with Christ and raised with Him too,
> What is there left for me to do?
> Simply to cease from struggle and strife,
> Simply to walk in newness of life."

In private life in Chicago Mr. Harper was bright and joyful, and though at times he was ill and suffered great pain, which was aggravated by over-work, he gloried in his weakness, because thereby the power of Christ was manifested in him.

In any spare time he had he was at the disposal of those who came, as many did each day, some to confess sin, and to be helped, guided, and prayed with.

He was a loving, sympathetic listener to many tales of sorrow and wrongdoing, and nothing was a trouble to him, and nothing a sacrifice if by any means he might save some.

His preparation for all this service was in his prayer life. What was witnessed and shared of that was a never-to-be-forgotten privilege. Often after a hard day's work he would reach his room tired out and much in need of rest and sleep, but something else claimed him. Instead of retiring he threw himself on his knees at the bedside, and by the hour he poured out his soul in agonizing prayer to God that salvation and blessing might come to those in Chicago, and

London, and Scotland, who were refusing the message of the Spirit. Friends were mentioned by name – those with whom he had been associated in Gospel work during the years of his ministry, and many as well about whose salvation he was concerned. There was a touch of softness and love and intimacy in the very tones of his voice as, in prayer, he used the beloved name, "Lord Jesus." It was evident that even then our brother had gone far into the presence of his Lord. Then ceasing prayer for a time, he would turn to the Word. The teaching that fell from his lips was wonderful as he gave expression to some new unfolding of truth which the "Lord Jesus" had just given him. The Lord, the Spirit, spoke through him indeed.

It is difficult for us to see why, just as a larger field of usefulness seemed to be opening out to him, the ministry of our brother should have been brought to an end. But we know that our God doeth all things well, and there we rest.

John Harper has "gone before" us to the larger service May his God and ours make us faithful as he was while we still labour here.

"Greater love hath no man than this, that a man lay down his life for his friends." (John 15:13).

Tribute - Mr Robert Logan, Evangelist

The sudden and unexpected end of our beloved brother, Mr. Harper, came to those of us who knew him and loved him as a staggering blow, and even yet we feel it difficult to think of him as having departed from the scene of his zealous, self-sacrificing, and fruitful labours. But we bow before the wisdom of the Divine Will that has permitted his removal. We shall know and understand the reason when the mists have rolled away. Absent from the body, he is now at home with the Lord, whom he supremely loved and faithfully served. The path of our brother was as "the shining light that shineth more and more unto the perfect day."

Mr. Harper was a strong man. He was strong in his love to the brethren. The grip of his kindly hand and his brotherly salutation were always cheering. He was strong in his love and reverence for the Bible. His progress in Bible study and Bible knowledge was very striking.

He was strong in his love for prayer. He knew as few men seemed to know that true power with men must be preceded with communion with God. Hence with him it was not the ordinary ten or fifteen minutes of waiting upon God. He spent hours in persistent wrestling with God in prayer for the salvation of perishing souls. Oh for a mighty increase of such intercessors!

He was strong in his love for the perishing. He had an intense love for souls. He was eager for the sanctification of saints. But oh! how he burned, prayed, laboured and wept for the conversion of sinners; and, blessed be God, great numbers were led to the Saviour's feet through his consecrated efforts.

He was strong in his love for the Saviour who died for him. He lived, walked, prayed and preached under the sense of an overwhelming version of Calvary. Hence Christ and Him crucified was ever his theme. To him the name of Jesus was sweet, sacred, and precious. May his mantle fall upon not a few of us so that we may successfully run the race that is set before us, until the day dawn when we shall meet to part no more.

Tribute - Mr. Alex Galbraith Seamen's Missionary, Glasgow

My acquaintance and fellowship with dear brother John Harper, whom I loved in the Lord, goes back for at least twelve or fourteen years, when in the beginning of His work for God on the Paisley Road (Gordon Halls), I had the joy of getting to know him and help him in the work there, and ever after I was in touch with him while in the city. My first impression on meeting him was this: That he was a man of great sympathy, who loved his Lord supremely, and was ready to help all who required help, and one whom Acts 11:24 describes accurately: "a good man, and full of the Holy Ghost, and of faith;" and right along ever after I saw the man develop and grow spiritually, in zeal for the souls of men, and in loyalty to Christ and His truth. My last communication from him was about a week before he appeared at the Noon Meeting in March for the last time, and the contents of his letter were mainly along the lines of urging to incessant activity for the ingathering of the lost, and the upbuiding of the saints, and encouraging myself personally to go on in the work among the fallen and the outcast; and the tenderness of his words of counsel and encouragement are with me still.

We had frequent private interviews in relation to the work of God, and I always found in him a friend and a brother of the highest type, who spoke evil of no man, but who was ever ready to do what he could for the furtherance of the Kingdom of God. I feel more than I can write.

10

A Man used by God

John Harper was a soul-winner. Here follows testimonies from converts he led to Christ

How I was led to Christ

Saturday, 9th August, 1902, was a day of great rejoicing on earth, because on that day our late King Edward was coronated amidst pomp and pageantry, and London was the centre of hundreds of representatives of other nations who were present at the magnificent event. The day following, Sabbath, 10th August, 1902, was a day of great rejoicing to me, because on that day my wife and I coronated Jesus Christ, and owned him King of our lives.

Work had being going on for about a year before this in the little "tin kirk," as the corrugated iron church (in which were held the services of the Paisley Road Baptist Church, under the ministry of Pastor John Harper), was called. The services were well attended, and very aggressive work was being carried on in the open-air just before our conversion. We had never been in a Baptist Church in our lives, but had seen Mr. Harper in the centre of his workers at the open-air meeting, at the corner of Plantation Street and Paisley Road, several times as we went up the street to Paisley Road. On Friday night, 7th

August, 1902, two workers from the Baptist Church knocked at the door of my wife's mother's house (we were not married then) and invited her to the Gospel Meeting in the iron church on Sabbath night, at 6.30. When I went to see her on the Saturday night she told me of the visit, and asked me if I would care to go with her. I usually attended another church, and did not much care about leaving our own church for a night even, and going to another. However, I consented, and the next night found me for the first time inside a Baptist Church. It was crowded. We received a hearty handshake from two deacons at the door, and a hymn book was put into our hands. The singing was hearty, with no stiffness about it. But the sermon – well, I don't know what the preacher said, but I remember his text: "He feedeth on ashes" (Isaiah 44:20). Pastor Harper was the preacher, and oh! how he did preach. Every word cut, and I felt convicted of sin, and knew there and then that I needed salvation. Not a word do I remember of the sermon, but the earnestness and burning passion of the preacher arrested me. I had never heard preaching like it, so powerful and so pleading, that when the sermon was over and a young man and young woman got up and sang the sweet duet, "Covered by the Blood of Jesus," I drank in the words of the hymn as a thirsty traveler under a burning sun drinks the clear sparkling water from the spring at the wayside. Little did I know that I was beginning to drink of that Living Water from the Eternal Spring, which, if a man drink of, he will never thirst again. The duet was finished, and a time of prayer followed. Then Mr. Harper asked for all those who wanted to trust Jesus Christ as their own personal Saviour to raise their hand, and mine went up. I knew I was a sinner. I knew I needed Christ. I knew enough of the Bible to be aware of the fact that I required to be converted before I could enter the Kingdom of Heaven. My parents both were Christians, and had taught me to read the Bible and say my prayers, go to church regularly, and to believe in a future state. I was a regular attender at church. No matter whether I was at a dance all Friday night, or at a football match on the Saturday afternoon, or at the theatre on the Saturday night, yet Sabbath forenoon found me at my usual place in the church. But that memorable 10th August found me stricken in soul before God and ripe for salvation. After my hand was raised I settled the question of my soul's salvation by accepting Jesus Christ as my Saviour. No one spoke to me. No one prayed with me. No one read texts to me. The transaction took place between my Lord and me, and it was blessedly real. Don't tell me a man does not know that he is saved, or when he gets saved. I knew that Sabbath night, sitting on the third back seat of the church, at the preacher's right hand, that my sins were forgiven, and I was born of God. Jesus can speak the world of peace to a soul. In the after meeting a dear brother who is now in glory came up to my wife and asked her if she was trusting Jesus. She said, "No." Then he spoke to her the Words of Life, but still she could not see the truth of salvation. He left speaking to her for a moment and turned to me and asked if I was saved. I said, "Yes," and my wife nearly took a fit. "That's not true," she said. She thought I had just said so to get rid of the man. She could not understand how I could be saved seeing no one spoke to me, nor read the Bible to me. But the Spirit of God had spoken to me. The Christian brother asked me how long it was since I trusted Christ, and I said, "When I raised my hand at the first meeting." He then turned again to my wife, told her of his conversation, and while telling her this, the light broke in, and she too was saved. Praise God for His wondrous love and grace. Both saved the same night. That is over nine years ago, and from that to this we have gone on our way, "Kept by the power of God, through faith, unto salvation." Three months afterwards we were baptized on our confession of faith in the Lord Jesus Christ, by Pastor Harper, and received into fellowship, and have continued in fellowship with the Church at Paisley Road since then. We have often thanked God that He led us to Paisley Road Baptist Church that night, 10th August, 1902, and that he privileged us to have ever known Mr. Harper. How he watched over us, praying for us, feeding us "on the finest of the wheat and honey from the rock," and carefully and wisely counseling us. We owe all we are, humanly speaking, to the inspiration that came from his consecrated life, and our only desire is to follow on to know the Lord, walking humbly and prayerfully before our God, so that He may be honoured and glorified by our daily lives. Our hearts were stricken when we heard of his tragic end, and yet methinks he would rather have been taken away suddenly than lie on a bed with a lingering illness. He has now entered into his rest, and his works do follow him. But the memory of his life will be an inspiration to all that knew him, and his burning zeal, yearning passion, loyal devotion, and intense earnestness cannot but have left their stamp upon those who sat under his ministry. Farewell, dear pastor, and father in the Gospel, may your children seek to walk worthy of the vocation unto which they are called. May the truths you have so often preached bear fruit in their lives. May your example of holy abandonment to the Will of God emulate others to follow, even as you followed Christ. And may your eyes even now rest on us all seeking to do the Will of God, and going on unto perfection. And yet it is not "Farewell," but only "Good-night." A few more days and then we'll all meet to part no more in that land of song and joy, where there are no more partings, and no more tears, no more pain, and no more sorrow, no more death, and no more sin. Thank God, no more sin.

"Until the day dawns and the shadows flee away."
"Sleep on beloved, sleep and take thy rest,
Lay down thy head upon thy Saviour's breast,
We loved thee well – but Jesus loves thee best,
Good-night. Good-night. Good-night."
"They that be wise shall shine as the brightness of the firmament, and they that turn many to righteousness, as the stars for ever and ever."
P.C.M.

"Behold God is my Salvation"

As a brand plucked from the burning I am thankful to God for His long-suffering and mercy, in that He did not cut me off in my sins. I had gone about as far as a man could go in the pleasures and follies of sin in drinking and gambling, and had on several occasions broken up my home and well-nigh ruined my business. It was while I was thus running on in my wild career that I was apprehended by the grace of God. On Saturday night, 6th November, 1897, I was as drunk as I could be, and on the Sunday night following was reaping what I had sowed. To while way the time I took a walk along Paisley Road with a friend who introduced me to two of the church members of the Baptist Church which had been formed about two months before, with Mr. Harper as pastor. For the first time in my life I was dealt with about my soul, and that night I was brought to a knowledge of the truth, being enabled from the heart to say, "I will trust, and not be afraid." Since then I have been a wonder unto many. God Himself wrought the change. That night my wife was also enabled to close in with offered mercy, and since then we have journeyed to Zion together. Instead of strong drink being followed after, I am satisfied with the living water which springs up into everlasting life. Instead of gambling and worrying about what I might win I have, by the grace of God, found the winner in Jesus Christ. Instead of blaspheming and using profane language I have a new song in my mouth. God has kept me by His grace for fourteen and a half years. To Him be all the glory. I am saved by grace through faith in Jesus who finished the work of my redemption on the Cross. There is one Mediator between God and men, the Man Christ Jesus, and I believe in Him. Praise His Holy Name.

J.B.

"Could not save myself"

My heart's desire and prayer to God is that some man who, like myself, has had the bitter and humiliating experience of innumerable trials and failures to lift himself out of sin, may on reading this humble testimony, trust Jesus Christ the only Saviour, and join with me in His praises. I was a Roman Catholic by birth, education, training and profession, learned to drink and to indulge in many other sins as well. While still very young I joined the army where the drink passion grew stronger, and led a very loose life. I served my time, returned home with the drink habit stronger than ever. Both in the service and in civil life I made several attempts to break away from drunkenness and other sins by going to confession, taking pledges, making resolutions, etc., but all to no avail. I could not save myself, and I often thought, "What is the good of all these confessions, etc., when each time I am as bad and often worse than before?" until one Saturday night, the 14th January, 1905, I found myself in the Iron Church, Plantation Street, again under the influence of drink. It was a time of revival, and every one seemed so intensely happy. The service went on, but I can't tell much about what was taking place, only that I got very unhappy and convinced that I was a very great sinner, and had been leading a very bad life. Thank God, a Christian man took notice of me and came over and sat down beside me. He was the means in God's hand of leading me to the Saviour. But it was not without a painful struggle. Satan brought up every possible and impossible reason why I should not trust Christ as my Saviour. But when I trusted Him the joy and peace and sense of a new power more than made up for all. Without the slightest doubt or fear I felt and knew that I was saved, and, thank God, I know it now. "I am not all I ought to be, but I am not what I used to be." All I am I owe, under God, to our late dearly beloved and much lamented Pastor John Harper, who was to me a father and brother, watching over me, praying for me, and instructing me in the new life. Four days after my conversion my wife was led to the Saviour. Three months later we were baptized, and joined the Church. I am now one of the deacons, having been appointed to the office a few months ago.

H.P.

"Whosoever"

I was a poor helpless sinner, held by the power of strong drink and a blaspheming tongue. I tried to repent by going to Church and taking the pledge, but it proved of no avail. A special mission was being held in the Baptist Church, in Gordon Halls. I had a brother a member of the Church. Special prayer was made for me. God heard and answered prayer. By invitation I went to one of the services. At the close one of the deacons spoke to me and asked if I was saved, or would I like to be. He read to me John 3:16, and showed me that "whosoever" meant anyone and must mean me. I trusted Christ that night, 11th October, 1898. Mr. Harper came to the house next morning to see if I had confessed Christ, which I had done, and have done ever since. I am what I am by the grace of God. I owe very much to my dear late Pastor, Mr. Harper, for his teaching and inspiration, and for the encouragement he gave me to be out and out for God. I praise God for the privilege of sitting under him for 12 years, and for being engaged in the Lord's work with him during that time. I now hold the position of a deacon, I, who was once a poor drunkard and blasphemer. But I found mercy through the Lord Jesus Christ. "To God be all the glory, great things he hath done."

A.M'L.

"He is able to Save"

Thank God for His saving grace in lifting a poor sinner like me from the dunghill, and setting me among princes. I was brought up a Presbyterian, but had no knowledge of God's salvation. As a lad, when living in Greenock, I went into the spirit trade with the determination to avoid the drink in any form, and not to taste it. But I soon fell under its power and dominion, and became a confirmed drunkard. I got so used to it that I could drink all the day long, and yet one could hardly tell it on me. I was twelve years selling the cursed stuff behind a public-house counter, and all these years I did not go home a single night sober. I left the drink trade and went to a lemonade manufacturer. But that was as bad, as I supplied the public houses with aerated waters, and got drunk there as well. At the age of twenty-five I came to Glasgow and went into the employment of P.&W. McLelland, at Clutha Iron Works. But still I was a victim to strong drink. I was gripped by the giant evil, and could not get free of its power. One night, at New Year, 1901, I took very ill, and the doctor was sent for. He said I had only three hours to live. This then was the end of my drinking; three hours – and then hell. I knew that was where I was going to. I knew there was no hope, but yet I prayed that God would spare me, and I would stop drinking, and live a better life. He did spare me, and for two years after I struggled against my love for whisky and beer, but still drank wine. I determined to pay a visit to every church in Glasgow, to see if I could hear of something that would bring me rest and peace. One Sunday evening, 1st November, 1903, I found myself in the Baptist Church, in Plantation Street, and heard Mr. Harper preach. A young lady sang "Over the dead line," and I felt that if I did not accept Jesus Christ I would pass over that dead line and be lost. No one spoke to me. I was so awakened to my need of Christ, that I knew all I had to do was accept Him as my Saviour. I did so, and now after eight and a half years of victory over

drink and sin I can say that God's Word is true, "If any man be in Christ he is a new creature, old things are passed away; behold, all things are become new" (II Cor. 5:17). I was in a new world. The drink desire was gone. Peace filled my soul. I knew from the moment I said, "Lord, I'll trust Thee, sink or swim, I'll trust Thee," that I was saved, and, thank God, I have been kept ever since by His mighty power and grace. About a year after, I was baptized, and joined the Church. I am now a deacon in the Church. Oh! what grace that transforms a poor drunkard a seller of whisky, and a deep-dyed sinner, such as I was, into a son of God and a child of His love. All I owe in my spiritual life I owe to the influence and teaching of Mr. Harper, who taught me the things of God, and whose life was an inspiration to me. May God help some poor drunkard to trust in my Saviour, and find that "He is able to dave to the uttermost all who come to God by Him."
J.C.S.

"His Grace is Sufficient"

I just want to give my humble testimony to the saving and keeping power of the Lord Jesus Christ, who has kept me by his grace for nearly fifteen years. It was on the 27th October, 1897, mother was giving a Hallowe'en party, and I was asked to bring up my sweetheart for her tea. Little did I think that it was for the purpose of getting me into touch with Mr. Harper that the party had been arranged. At length the night came, and we were all gathered in the room, and to my great surprise who did I see in the room but Mr. Harper and several members of the Church (one of them now the senior deacon of the Church). My mother was a member of the Church, being amongst the first number that was at the start of the Church in the Gordon Halls. Of course, I knew what would happen after tea – I would be spoken to about my soul. Well, we had our tea, and then after a little conversation I thought it was time for me to get out. It was getting too warm for me, so I got up to get my cap, but could not find it. It had been removed from its place. But I went out with my bare head, but I did not stop long as it was a cold night, so I had to go back to the house again, for the purpose of getting some covering for my head. Little did I think I was to get a covering for my sins. When I got to the house, an elderly brother got hold of me and spoke to me about Christ. In the corner of the room Mr. Harper was dealing with my sweetheart about her soul. Shortly after, Mr. Harper engaged in prayer thanking God for her decision. I then threw down the arms of rebellion and accepted Christ also as my Saviour and Lord. The Scriptures we saw the light through were Isaiah 53:5, "All we like sheep," etc., and Romans 10:9, "If thou shalt confess with thy mouth the Lord Jesus," etc. That eventful night will never be erased from our memories, and we were baptized shortly afterwards, and joined the Church. After over fourteen year's experience of Christ's love and salvation we can say that His grace is sufficient for us, and His strength is made perfect in weakness. What we are in the Christian life we owe to our late lamented pastor, Mr. Harper, whose godly life and holy example proved such a help to us, and who looked after us as carefully as a father after his children, and brought us to love the study of Scripture and the joy of waiting upon God in prayer. Would to God I could pray like him, and now that he is in the presence of the Lord whom he so much loved and so loyally served, our only desire is to follow in his steps even as he followed Christ.

C.B. and Mrs. B.

"Behold, I stand at the door"

On the Sabbath evening of July 4, 1897, I went to hear Mr. Harper. The text he spoke from was Revelation 3:20, "Behold I stand at the door and knock." I had been convicted for some time, and, as Mr. Harper went on, my conviction deepened, and I saw I needed a Saviour. There I surrendered my all, and I have been going on my way rejoicing ever since. It has not always been sunshine, but Christ is all in all to me. I am a member of Paisley Road Baptist Church, and so is my wife.

On the Sabbath evening of 27th June, 1897, I went to the Boilermakers' Hall, Govan, where Pastor Harper was then preaching, and the text he spoke from was John 3:36. I was convicted of sin, saw my need of a Saviour, and there and then surrendered to Christ.

11

A Man of Intercession

Wanted – Intercessors! Part of an address delivered at the Moody Church, Chicago

Vision, compassion, intercession – these are three great links in the golden chain of redemptive service. How clearly you can see them in the saving ministry and life service of our Lord Jesus Himself. He saw the multitudes as sheep without a shepherd – scattered, torn, bruised, and bleeding – and if that was the vision before His eyes when He looked on a multitude from the quiet religious villages of Galilee, where the people were moral in their habits of life, and not sunken with drink and manifold vice, what would be the vision before Him if He looked today on Chicago?

With that vision His heart was moved with compassion, agitated with deep feeling – agonised within Him, would be a better word. He had compassion on them, taking their pain and sorrow up into His own heart of love, and with that love-swept spirit He turns to His disciples and says, "Pray ye," and on every possible occasion slips off Himself to the lonely mountain side to spend the night or early morning hours in prayer.

Beloved, how few of us have the Master's vision, and hence, how few of us have the compassion-filled heart, the consequent ministry of intercession! If any one conviction has laid hold of my spirit more than another, and has held it in a grasp as solemn as eternity for some years past, it is that the overwhelming need of the church and the doomed world is intercessors – not so much preachers however great that need is – but men of the mountain solitude and midnight watch, who know how to stand between God and men, in fasting and prayer; and who will not leave the throne of grace until from His presence will go forth times of refreshing and salvation that will make His name a praise in the earth.

Then will be given to the church, preachers with the tongues of fire, and workers mantled with His power; and the whole awakened Spirit-filled church will become the instrument of our glorified Lord in awakening a godless world to the conviction of sin and sense of need of the atoning blood, and to the fear of coming wrath.

A very little while and He will come, and the door will be shut, and the doom of Christendom sealed. Only a brief season can remain for us all. But what may not be done in these quickly passing days! What seasons of prayer and intercession may we not have! What sacrifices for Him may we not make! What power from the throne may we not receive! What scenes of blessing may we not witness in the gathering out of the last members of the body of Christ from this doomed and darkening world, while upon it the night shadows of coming judgment are falling fast!

Beyond this little while there will be the glory of His presence, the glad reunion with the loved, the thrilling "well done" of the Master at His judgment seat – the entering in, to go out no more forever.
But – but – there will be no more opportunity of praying lost souls to His feet and winning them to His heart forever.

"Perishing, perishing, thou wast not willing;
Master, forgive and inspire us anew;
Banish our worldliness, help us forever
To live with eternity's values in view."

12

A Man to be Remembered

Tribute - Pastor Wm Wright, Denny

Denny and surrounding district are much indebted to God for the gift of Mr. John Harper.The connecting link between him and Denny was a young man from Castlecary, and thereby in the providence of God John Harper was led to conduct a mission in Denny fully eleven years ago, in which his brother George also assisted. God signally blessed the effort in leading souls to decision for Christ, and also in the enlightening of ourselves in the manner in which the work of God ought to be carried on. I felt there was a manifestation of Christ in his life that I had not known before. We had on one occasion a conversation about the indwelling of Christ, and he suggested our need of being "strengthened with might by His Spirit in the inner man," that Christ might dwell in our hearts by faith. Early in life he had experienced this strengthening process, and when he came to Denny it was seen in a marvellous degree.

He believed in having the text he was to preach from direct from God, and I have seen his soul in great trouble until he had the witness of the Holy Spirit in regard to the passage of Scripture he was to expound. He also had the stamp of heaven on the title he gave to the subjects he preached about, and his divisions were masterly. Denny is not easily moved, but when he had the town placarded with bills asking "Is there a hell?" it made some stop and think. He announced one subject that has remained with me: "The hardest thing in the world," which he proved to be to go to hell, from II Peter 3 and 9, as the sinner has to go there against the will of God.

In September, 1910, he delivered one of the freshest and most hopeful messages I have ever heard. The subject was "Green fields and white fields." The fields were green in the eyes of the disciples, they were white to the harvest in the eyes of our Lord. In delivering a mighty message from God during the same short mission, he raised a question for the evolutionists to answer, in this form: "If the status of human character is continually rising, how is it that the One Who is almost universally recognized as the perfect man, Jesus, existed nearly nineteen hundred years ago?"

How liberally the Lord laid to his hand! Some so-called authorities will say if a man prepares and preaches one or two good sermons in a week he has done sufficient. Any more would mean imperfect and inefficient work. Our brother, Mr. Harper, would sometimes face the same audience many times in a week, pretty regularly six times, without repeating himself. I have heard him going over a division of a subject for a women's meeting that I was inclined to think at the time might have been reserved for a special conference.

Mr. Spurgeon remarks in one of his sermons that if a man has a personal conflict with Satan it will be a red letter day in his history. Along that line of things Mr. Harper had many red letter days and nights. It was his firm conviction that Satan would have killed him if he could. He was continually conscious, especially in the latter years of his ministry, of the conflict going on in every service between the powers of light and the powers of darkness. He gave me a little hint personally last September in London that has been very helpful to my soul on this effect: "The devil cannot touch you on resurrection ground." Although often assailed by Satan, he enjoyed in a superlative degree the rest of God.

Nine years ago I asked him the question, "In the Gospel what takes the place of the fourth commandment?" His instant reply was, "The rest of God."

To the uninitiated his removing from Glasgow to London looked like a wrong step, but a revived church in London, and other churches influenced for good, proved it to be the mind of the Spirit which he had followed in leaving Paisley Road for Walworth Road.

My parting with him near the station at Old Cumnock, last March, was an incident worth remembering. We agreed to give each other a text. I gave him the one, "Feed my lambs," which led him to make this noteworthy statement: When he was in Chicago he was earnestly engaged in secret prayer, when God, by His Holy Spirit, give the assurance to him that his little daughter, six yeas of age, was a Christian. I thanked God and him most sincerely for the beautiful story, and all the more because I am convinced that this is where many are up against the will of God today, in not recognizing believing children as the lambs of the flock.

The text he gave me was one that had been much in his mind for a considerable time, "He that doeth the will of God abideth for ever." (I John 2:17)

13

Lasting Lessons from Looking Back

In 1898, fourteen years before the RMS Titanic made her maiden voyage, Morgan Robertson, a well-known American novelist, published a book entitled, *FUTILITY: The Wreck of the Titan*. The parallels between the Titan and the Titanic are amazing.

The book told a fictitious story of an "unsinkable" British ocean liner, which like the Titanic, was crossing the Atlantic but in the opposite direction, from west to east, from America to England.

Similar to the Titanic, this enormous ship was making the transatlantic crossing in the month of April with 3,000 passengers and crew. It was trying to cross the ocean in record time, and it too, near to midnight, struck an iceberg and sank. Not only were the ships' names very similar, but most on board also perished simply because there was a lack of lifeboats.

The similarities are remarkable. I think there are other parallels we can draw from the story of the sinking of the *RMS Titanic* and the Bible story of God's Unsinkable Ark which Noah built.

1. The folly of ignoring God in our lives.

On the day that the Titanic was launched one of the Belfast workers flippantly said, "Not even God could sink the *Titanic.*"

Alas, today there are too many who either deny the existence of God or feel they do not need Him in their lives. The Bible reminds us, "The fool hath said in his heart, 'There is no God'." This is not just a mental denial of an atheist. It is the fool who makes shipwreck by disregarding God in his life.

It was God who instructed Noah to build an ark. It was God who invited Noah into the ark. It was God who kept Noah and his family in the ark. Noah trusted in God.

2. The insufficiency of trusting in human efforts.

Following the underwater discovery of the hull of the Titanic in 1985, maritime experts established that the structural steel used in the Titanic's plates had become brittle at the icy temperatures of that tragic night. As a result, it took only a glancing blow to cause the 300 foot gash to open on the starboard hull.

The size, substance and structure of Noah's ark were all designed by God. Noah's security did not depend on his works or wisdom. God secured the ark. The prophet Jeremiah wrote; "Thus saith the LORD; Cursed be the man that trusteth in man and maketh flesh his arm, and whose heart departeth from the LORD. . . Blessed is the man that trusteth in the LORD, and whose hope the LORD is" (Jeremiah 17:5, 7).

3. The uncertainty of human life.

All who embarked on the *Titanic* expected to reach the United States before the week was over. Sadly, less than one third of those on board the great ship reached their destination. The wisest king in the Bible spoke about the uncertainty of life when he said, "Boast not thyself of tomorrow; for thou knowest not what a day may bring forth" (Proverbs 27:1).

By the end of that week in April 1912, 1503 souls arrived in the great eternity. The Bible says, "It is appointed unto men once to die, but after this the judgment" (Hebrews 9:27).

Noah knew that God loved him. He also recognized that one day he would have to meet God, the righteous Judge. That is why we read of him in Hebrews 11:7: "By faith Noah, being warned of God of things not seen as yet, moved with fear, prepared an ark to the saving of his house; by the which he condemned the world, and became heir of the righteousness which is by faith." Noah entered the ark because he was trusting in God.

4. The sufficiency of God's salvation.

It is thought that the *Titanic* was inadequately equipped for the major disaster that sealed its fate. They did not expect disaster; therefore, they were not prepared. There were not sufficient life boats to carry all the people on board. Furthermore, not all the lifeboats carried a full capacity of people.

The ark which Noah constructed was God's lifeboat. On board there was ample room for all who would enter. Alas, only eight people accepted God's invitation to enter the ark; and therefore, only eight were saved.

The Bible says of Jesus Christ, "Wherefore he is able also to save them to the uttermost that come unto God by him, seeing he ever liveth to make intercession for them (Hebrews 7:25). On the cross the Lord Jesus Christ made one offering for sin forever. He invites you to come to the cross and find salvation. There is adequate room at the cross for you.

5. The simplicity and security of the gospel of Jesus Christ

While on board the *Titanic* and even in the freezing waters of the North Atlantic, John Harper had one simple but sure message for men and women on the slippery decks or when facing imminent death in the water. To lost souls all around him he repeated the words of the apostle Paul: "Believe on the Lord Jesus Christ, and thou shalt be saved."

God's invitation to Noah and his family was expressed with the word, "come". God said to Noah, "Come thou and all thy house into the ark." Jesus Christ also invites us to come to Him. He says, "Come unto me, all ye that labour and are heavy laden, and I will give you rest" (Matthew 11:28).

6. The urgency of trusting in Jesus Christ

When Dr Robert Ballard discovered the wreckage of the Titanic at a depth of 13000 feet on the ocean bed in 1985 he was overwhelmed. He had searched for it for several years. After briefly filming the wreckage it is reported that he scratched on the rusty hull, "I will return."

That is the promise that Jesus Christ has left for us. Jesus said, "I will come again." The coming of our blessed Lord will be the greatest rescue mission of all time. The Bible says that the dead in Christ shall rise first, then we which are alive and remain, shall be caught up together with them to meet the Lord in the air and so shall we ever be with the Lord. What a day that is going to be.

However, not only is Jesus coming for His own, judgement is also coming for those who are out of Christ. The Bible says that

God "hath appointed a day, in the which he will judge the world in righteousness by that man whom he hath ordained; whereof he hath given assurance unto all men, in that he hath raised him from the dead."

Be sure that you are ready for that day. Let me repeat again the testimony of John Harper's last convert:

On that terrible night when the *RMS Titanic* was sinking a young man was struggling in the freezing waters like many despairing passengers. He laid hold of a floating object and clung to it for dear life. Above the groans and shrieks of the terrified passengers he could hear a voice calling to him, "Is your soul saved?"

The young man answered, "I fear it is not."

"Then," called out John Harper, "Believe on the Lord Jesus Christ, and thou shalt be saved." With that Harper was carried away by the current. Even then he could hear the preacher still calling out to others, "Believe on the Lord Jesus Christ, and thou shalt be saved."

The young man later said, "There and then, with two miles of water beneath me, I believed on Christ and was saved. I was John Harper's last convert."

Learn these lessons from the *Titanic*. Today, if you hear His voice, harden not your heart. This is the day of salvation.

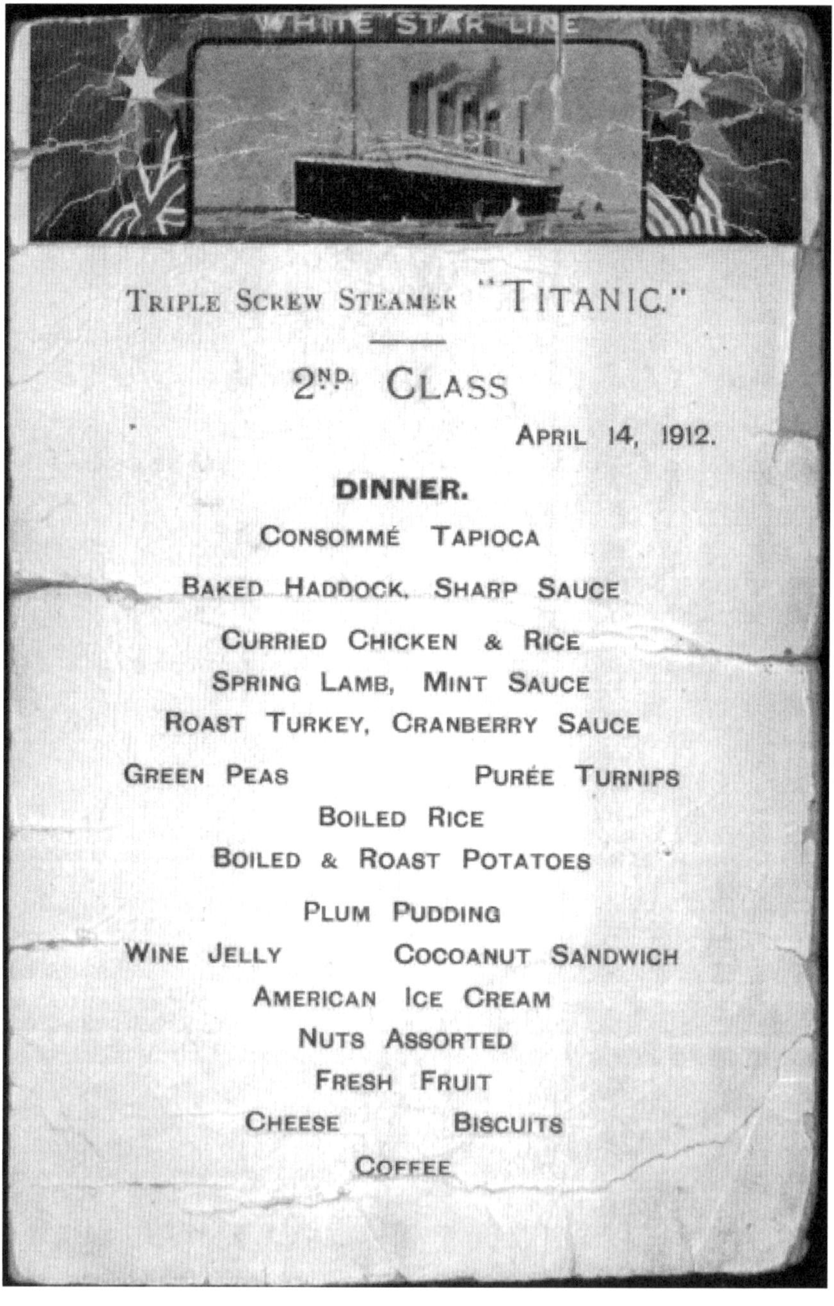

WHITE STAR LINE

TRIPLE SCREW STEAMER "TITANIC."

2ND. CLASS

APRIL 14, 1912.

DINNER.

CONSOMMÉ TAPIOCA

BAKED HADDOCK, SHARP SAUCE

CURRIED CHICKEN & RICE

SPRING LAMB, MINT SAUCE

ROAST TURKEY, CRANBERRY SAUCE

GREEN PEAS PURÉE TURNIPS

BOILED RICE

BOILED & ROAST POTATOES

PLUM PUDDING

WINE JELLY COCOANUT SANDWICH

AMERICAN ICE CREAM

NUTS ASSORTED

FRESH FRUIT

CHEESE BISCUITS

COFFEE

The Boston Daily Globe.
TITANIC SINKS, 1500 DIE
Carpathia Picks Up 675 Out of 2200---Races for New York---Survivors Mostly Women and Children.
POLICE ORDER DORR'S ARREST
Lynn Chief Accuses Him of the Murder of George E. Marsh
Suspect Said to Have Left Boston Thursday Night—Auto Found Here.
Giant Steamer Goes Down Before Help Arrives.
Virginian or Parisian May Have Some Survivors
White Star Officials Admit "Horrible Loss of Life".

The GREATEST WRECK in HISTORY

THE LOSS OF THE WHITE STAR TITANIC

THE LARGEST SHIP IN THE WORLD, WHICH SANK ON ITS MAIDEN VOYAGE WITH A LOSS OF 1635 LIVES

TITANIC
DISASTER
GREAT LOSS
OF LIFE
EVENING NEWS

New Titanic interpretation centre in Belfast